S0-EFO-569

# The PRONUNCIATION

# of Standard American

# ENGLISH

JAMES G. LUTER, JR., PH.D.

GARRETT
PUBLISHING
COMPANY

GRANADA HILLS, CALIFORNIA

ISBN 0-939085-00-3

Printed and bound in the United States of America

# ACKNOWLEDGEMENTS

I wish to express my gratitude to my students for their inspiration, to my colleagues for their patience, understanding and willing eyes and ears. Much thanks is also due to my family and friends who have helped greatly in the final stages of preparation.

# PREFACE

The process of acquiring a new language has many steps. You learn to listen and to read, to speak and to write. Often, you study a new alphabet and the ways of writing and pronouncing its letters. You work with spelling and grammar. You develop a new vocabulary and learn idioms and slang. Your ability to communicate in the new tongue grows with time and experience. It is an exciting and rewarding process.

Each language has certain characteristics which give learners trouble. Some have complicated grammar such as Spanish and German. Others, like Chinese, have writing systems which are difficult to learn. Pronunciation of words is a problem with yet others, most especially with English.

This book was designed to assist those who struggle with speaking American English. It concentrates on the areas which cause most learners of the language great difficulty: stress, intonation, articulation and pronunciation. It provides a simple, natural approach to acquiring these important skills.

The first three chapters explain the basic workings of the speech mechanism, discuss the use of pronunciation guides and the characteristics of stress and intonation. The next three chapters deal with the sounds of English. Each has word lists, sentences, and, for fun, a tongue twister and a limerick as practice material. The final chapters cover sound blends and word endings.

Each of the lessons contain ten sentences which introduce a topic in either story or essay form. These can be used to stimulate conversation and classroom discussion. Each is arranged in facing pages, with the descriptive material on the left and the practice sets on the right. Diagrams of the mouth are provided for each of the lessons on sounds to assist you with their formation.

We hope that you will enjoy working with this text as much as we have enjoyed putting it together.

James G. Luter, Jr., Ph.D.,
Granada Hills, California

# TABLE OF CONTENTS

# INTRODUCTION

This book is written to help persons learning American English as a second language. It is designed specifically for those who have good English reading and writing ability, but who need to improve their speaking skills.

There is a saying, common in the Armed Forces, that there are three ways of doing something: the right way, the wrong way and the Army way. Second language speech can be similarly described. There is right speech, wrong speech and learner's speech, which is usually somewhere in the middle.

The language student with a new word is like a child with a new toy. He/she tries to use it before learning how. Both have similar results: broken toys and destroyed words. If a word is said right the first time, there is no problem. If not, a wrong pronunciation is learned. It must later be unlearned and corrected, a much harder task.

## THE RIGHT WAY

The best way for learning to speak a second language is one most similar to that used for the first: by listening to and imitating native speakers.

Your first language was acquired in a remarkably short period of time, considering the difficulty of the task. As an infant, you knew a few simple words by the end of your first year. By the end of your fourth year, however, you were able to converse easily. You were following a _natural_ pattern of development: you learned simple sounds and words first, followed by more complex ones as your needs and abilities grew. You heard and imitated those around you. They let you know by their reactions whether or not you had communicated successfully. Sometimes, you had to make corrections to produce speech accurately, but in those few years, you mastered the language.

Learning a second language usually follows a different pattern. If you studied English in your native land, you learned to speak it by imitating a teacher. In most cases, that person spoke English with the accent of your country. The English you speak, therefore, is accented in the same way. If you learned after coming to the United States, you fared no better. Your most frequent contacts were other immigrants. You learned from each other and reinforced the same errors again and again. As a result, you have developed a number of incorrect speech habits.

To assist you in developing correct speech skills, the best pattern to follow is one most similar to the way you learned your first language. You must listen to an appropriate model, imitate what you hear and obtain a reaction in order to determine success or to make corrections.

You will have to learn to:
(1) Recognize and produce the new speech sounds which are new to **you** or produced differently in your old language.
(2) Combine the new sounds into words.
(3) Use correctly pronounced words in conversation.
(4) Recognize and produce correct American stress and intonation patterns.

All of these skills have to be learned separately at first and then be combined under controlled conditions for improvement to take place.

2

## STANDARD AMERICAN ENGLISH

There are dozens of dialects spoken in the United States. The most useful, however, is called Standard American English. It is spoken by approximately fifty (50) percent of the college trained population of this country, and is the one most commonly heard on television and radio. For these reasons, it is the dialect used in this text. It is also presented on the cassette recordings which accompany it.

## SPELLING AND SOUNDS

English is not spelled phonetically, that is, there is often little relation between a specific letter in a word and the sound that it represents. Indeed, the way a word is spelled may indicate nearly nothing about the way it is said. For this reason, systems of symbols have been developed to represent English pronunciation. These are usually noted in the pronunciation guides of the various dictionaries. Unfortunately for you, no two dictionaries use exactly the same system. Textbook writers often develop their own systems, which may also be unique. In some cases, you may have to learn two separate sound alphabets, one to read the book and one to use a dictionary.

## DICTIONARIES

In this text, you will see the symbol systems from three different dictionaries:

1.  Kenyon and Knott, A PRONOUNCING DICTIONARY OF AMERICAN ENGLISH, Mirriam Webster, Inc., Springfield, Mass., 1953.

2.  DICTIONARY OF AMERICAN ENGLISH, A DICTIONARY FOR LEARNERS OF ENGLISH, Longman, Inc., New York, 1983.

3.  AMERICAN HERITAGE DICTIONARY, American Heritage Publishing Company and Houghton Mifflin Co., New York, 1983.

Each of these dictionaries has specific features which make them useful to the learner of English.

Each also has drawbacks which make them somewhat of a problem. The Kenyon and Knott book contains pronunciations for about 40,000 words. It is especially useful for proper nouns and names. It does not have definitions, however, just pronunciations and it does not contain the newly coined words derived from the recent advances in space and computer technology.

The Longman dictionary has a similar number of words with their pronunciations and definitions. It also contains a useful study guide for those new to the use of dictionaries. It contains, however, no place or personal names. Both of these dictionaries use modifications of the International Phonetic Alphabet to indicate pronunciation.

The American Heritage Dictionary uses diacritic markings instead of phonetic symbols in its pronunciation guide. It contains definitions, place and proper names, and has pictures of many common objects. It is one of the most useful diacritic dictionaries available.

In the descriptive sections of this book, the IPA symbols of Kenyon and Knott have been used. With minor differences, they are quite similar to those of the Longman Dictionary. Its vowel and diphthong symbols are very different from those in the American Heritage Dictionary, but many of the consonants symbols are quite similar.

## AUDIO CASSETTES

Audio cassette recordings are available for your use with this book. They contain all of its practice material. They are recorded with space between each item so that you will have time to repeat one before the next is heard. They will prove valuable to you long after formal instruction is over. See Appendix A for suggestions as to how they can be used.

The cassettes may be ordered by using a form which can be found in the front of the book. If it is missing, write to the address on the copyright page and the publisher will send the appropriate information.

# CHAPTER 1

# THE SPEECH MECHANISM

Speech is produced as a result of the interaction among several areas of the human anatomy. The process is quite complex. For you to improve your speaking skills, however, you will need to have a working knowledge of the way the organs of speech act.

Speech, as are most human actions, is governed by the brain. Once you determine what you wish to say, the brain organizes the movements of certain parts of your body to produce the statements you need. The process is automatic, fortunately. You do not have to think about what you are doing, most of the time. You only think of the idea and the brain does the rest.

The brain sends its speech messages to three major areas of the body: <u>the breathing</u>, <u>the voicing</u> and <u>the articulating systems</u>. These three systems interact to produce the sounds and words of speech.

## THE BREATHING SYSTEM

Air is inhaled and exhaled by the action of the muscles of the abdomen and chest. For speech, our primary interest is in exhalation. Air is pushed out of the lungs by the action of two sets of muscles: (1) those which lie between the ribs, and (2) the abdominal muscles. The air moves up from the lungs

into the windpipe and through the <u>larynx</u> attached
above it. From there, it moves on to the throat,
mouth and/or nose.

## THE VOICING SYSTEM

The sound of the voice is the result of exhaled
air being pushed between the two <u>vocal folds</u> (often
called "vocal cords") which are attached to the inner
sides of the larynx. When they are brought together,
the moving air stream causes them to vibrate (this
vibration is similar to what happens at the neck of a
full rubber balloon when air is let out rapidly).

The vocal folds, when apart, form a "V" shaped
opening called the <u>glottis</u>. This is their breathing
position. When <u>phonating</u> (making sound), the glottis
is lightly closed so that the exhaled breath stream
causes the the vocal folds to flutter.

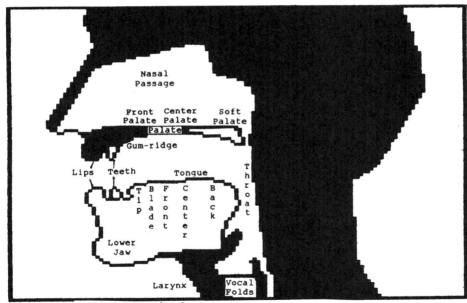

## Figure 1.1 - THE ARTICULATORS

## THE ARTICULATING SYSTEM

For speech, articulation is the process of moving
the speech muscles to produce the individual speech

sounds. It involves the organs of the throat and
mouth, including the <u>tongue,</u> <u>lips,</u> <u>teeth,</u> <u>gum-ridge,</u>
<u>palate,</u> <u>soft palate</u> and <u>lower jaw.</u>

The tongue is the most important of these organs.
It is the largest, most flexible and most complex of
the other speech structures. It is divided into
several areas: the <u>tongue-tip,</u> <u>blade,</u> <u>front,</u> <u>center</u>
and <u>back</u> (Figure 1.1).

The tongue-tip is the outer edge of the pointed
end of the tongue. The blade is the area immediately
behind the tip, while the front, center and back of
the tongue divide the remaining area into thirds.

The tongue front is curved toward the palate to
produce many sounds. The tip is touched to the teeth
or gum ridge for several others. The back of the
tongue is raised toward the soft palate for still
more. Each of the five areas of the tongue is used
in producing one or more speech sounds.


The lips form the fleshy, muscular, outer edges
of the mouth. Their shape may be changed or brought
in contact with the teeth in producing many sounds.

The teeth, of course, are not moved in producing
sounds. They provide a sharp edge past which air can
be forced. The result is a hissing type sound.

The gum-ridge is located directly behind the
upper front teeth. You can feel it by rubbing your
tongue-tip against the back of your teeth and then
pulling it up and back along the top of the mouth.
The tongue tip and blade contact the gum-ridge in the
production of several sounds.

The <u>palate</u> (the roof of the mouth) is divided
into two areas. They are the <u>front-palate</u> and
<u>center-palate.</u> They form the hard or bony surface
you can feel with your tongue behind the gum-ridge.
For certain sounds, the tongue is moved closer to or
farther from the palate.

The <u>soft palate</u> is a group of muscles attached to
the back of the palate. When raised, it prevents

exhaled air from entering the nasal passage, the case for most sounds. When lowered, it allows free passage of air into the nose. Like the hard palate, it provides a surface which the back of the tongue nears, or touches, in the production of various sounds.

The lower jaw is the bony an muscular structure lying below the tongue and lower teeth. Its movements open and close the mouth. It makes possible the wide range of adjustments needed for clear production of speech sounds.

## VOICING SPEECH SOUNDS

Each of the speech sounds we use is produced by combining various actions of the organs we have discussed. Some sounds, for example, are _voiced_ (made with vibration of the vocal folds). Others are _voiceless_ (made with no vocal fold vibration). For example, put your fingers on your throat and say: "mmmmmmmm." Your fingers will feel vibration. Then say: "ssssssss." You will feel no action. We say that the "m" sound is voiced and the "s" is voiceless.

## ARTICULATING SPEECH SOUNDS

Some speech sounds are made with the mouth fairly wide open, such as "ah." Others require that the mouth be nearly closed, such as "ee." Some have the tongue raised, others lowered. Some block the breath stream, others allow it to flow freely. Each sound is produced by a specific set of actions. In Chapters 4, 5 and 6, the various movements of the articulators will be discussed in detail.

## SUMMARY

Speech requires the coordinated movements of several organs of the body. The breathing mechanism and the vocal folds combine their actions in producing voice. The tongue, lips, lower jaw and soft palate move to specific positions for each separate sound. The learning of all these actions in your first language occurred naturally. Now, you will need much skill and concentration to acquire the new movement patterns of American English.

CHAPTER 2

# PHONETICS AND DIACRITICS

Some languages are described as <u>phonetic</u>. Each of their **letters represents only one sound.** Spanish and Greek are good examples of such languages. The spelling of their words tells you how to pronounce them.

English, however, is written with a 26 letter alphabet, but contains over 40 distinct speech sounds. As a result, it is often impossible to determine from looking at a word how it should be pronounced. Many letters are used to represent several different sounds. This is especially true among the vowels. There are five vowel letters, "a, e, i, o, and u." They are used to write 17 separate sounds.

Consider the following sentence: "Father talks about saving many stamps." Each word contains the letter "a," but each "a" represents a different vowel. Such a situation is definately confusing to the learner of English.

Look at the following word: "chuigh." You will not find it in the dictionary, but, considering the strangeness of English spelling, it could be a real word. To determine how to pronounce it, take the "ch" from "Chicago," the "ui" from "build" and the "gh" from "hiccough." In these words, the "ch" is produced like "sh," the "ui" like "i," and the "gh"

9

like "p." Therefore, "chuigh" is pronounced like "ship."

## NEW ALPHABETS

Because of such problems, many approaches have been made for the past 400 years to find a more acceptable way of indicating English pronunciation than its spelling. So far, no method has totally succeeded.

A number of attempts have been made to invent new English alphabets in which each letter represents only one sound. None have ever gone into general use, although one, the Deseret Alphabet, had limited success. It was developed by the Church of Jesus Christ of Latter Day Saints during the mid-1800s. At that time, in Utah, a large number of European immigrants were arriving. The church felt it necessary for them to learn English as rapidly as possible, so a new alphabet was used for several years in newspapers and school books. It proved helpful in teaching English. The arrival of other newspapers and the ready availability of books in regular print, however, caused the Deseret Alphabet to fall into disuse. Publishers did not want to print everything in two ways. Additionally, the people were not anxious to learn two systems of reading and writing.

## THE IPA

In the 1880's the International Phonetic Association was formed. One of its purposes was to develop an alphabet which could be used to write any word in any language. The result was the International Phonetic Alphabet (usually called the IPA). It forms the basis for the pronunciation guide in many dictionaries.

Other approaches to writing sounds include the placing of marks over existing alphabet letters. The marks (called diacritic marks) are used by many dictionary publishers.

If you look up a word in a dictionary using the IPA, you might see something like this: "learn-ing ['lɜ˞nɪŋ]." If you look in a dictionary using diacritic marks, it would look like this: "learn-ing (lûr'nĭng)."

Chart 2.1 provides a comparison of three systems for writing sounds. These symbols are used throughout the text. Study their similarities and differences. The first column contains key words which contain a specific speech sound. The second through fourth columns contain the corresponding symbols from three dictionaries: A PRONOUNCING DICTIONARY OF AMERICAN ENGLISH, Longman's DICTIONARY OF AMERICAN ENGLISH, and THE AMERICAN HERITAGE DICTIONARY. The first two are modifications of the IPA and the third is a diacritic marking system.

## PHONEMES

Language scholars refer to "speech sounds" as phonemes. Each phoneme has one or more characteristics which cause it to differ from the rest. Phonemes are are divided into three groups, vowels, diphthongs, and consonants. Each of these groups of phonemes differ in several ways from the others.

## VOWELS

Vowel sounds are the foundation for English words. All words contain at least one vowel and several are simply vowels alone, for example, "a," "I" and "oh." Vowel sounds are all produced with vocal fold vibration, that is, they are all voiced. The breath stream is neither squeezed through a narrow opening or blocked, as in the case of many consonants. The articulators do not go through large movements, as with the diphthongs and some consonants. The speech organs move relatively little while producing vowel sounds; the voiced breath stream flows freely from the mouth. Examples of vowel sounds are the "e" in "speech," or the "u" in "push."

## DIPHTHONGS

Diphthong sounds are blends of two vowels. The articulators move from the position of one to the

11

## Chart 2.1 - DICTIONARY SYMBOLS

| | KENYON AND KNOTT PRONOUNCING DICTIONARY | LONGMAN DICTIONARY OF AMERICAN ENGLISH | AMERICAN HERITAGE DICTIONARY |
|---|---|---|---|
| **VOWELS** | | | |
| EAT, SPEAK, THREE | [i] | /iʸ/ | ē |
| IS, DID | [ɪ] | /ɪ/ | ĭ |
| ATE, PAID, STAY | [e] | /eʸ/ | ā |
| ENTER, RED | [ɛ] | /ɛ/ | ĕ |
| APPLE, PLAN | [æ] | /æ/ | ă |
| ODD, STOP, SPA | [a] | /a/ | ä |
| ALL, BOUGHT, LAW | [ɔ] | /ɔ/ | ô |
| OLD, BOAT, KNOW | [o] | /oʷ/ | ō |
| BOOK | [ʊ] | /ʊ/ | o͝o |
| OODLES, SOUP, TWO | [u] | /uʷ/ | o͞o |
| EARLY, FIRST, SIR | [ɝ] | /ɝr/ | ûr |
| ANSWER, LATER | [ɚ] | /ər/ | ər |
| UP, FUN | [ʌ] | /ʌ/ | ŭ |
| ABOUT, DOZEN, AREA | [ə] | /ə/ | ə |
| **DIPHTHONGS** | | | |
| EYE, RICE, WHY | [aɪ] | /aɪ/ | ī |
| OIL, NOISE, TOY | [ɔɪ] | /ɔɪ/ | oi |
| OUT, POUND, NOW | [aʊ] | /aʊ/ | ou |

| | KENYON<br>AND KNOTT<br>PRONOUNCING<br>DICTIONARY | LONGMAN<br>DICTIONARY<br>OF AMERICAN<br>ENGLISH | AMERICAN<br>HERITAGE<br>DICTIONARY |
|---|---|---|---|

## CONSONANTS

| | KENYON | LONGMAN | AMERICAN |
|---|---|---|---|
| PUT, OPEN, TOP | [p] | /p/ | p |
| BACK, TABLE, RUB | [b] | /b/ | b |
| TIME, INTO, RIGHT | [t] | /t/ | t |
| DOOR, UNDER, BED | [d] | /d/ | d |
| CAT, TAKEN, LOOK | [k] | /k/ | k |
| GET, AGO, LEG | [g] | /g/ | g |
| FINE, AWFUL, LIFE | [f] | /f/ | f |
| VERY, EVER, LIVE | [v] | /v/ | v |
| THIN, BATHS, BOTH | [θ] | /θ/ | th |
| THE, OTHER, BATHE | [ð] | /ð/ | th |
| SUN, LESSON, RICE | [s] | /s/ | s |
| ZOO, EASY, WAS | [z] | /z/ | z |
| SHE, OCEAN, CASH | [ʃ] | /ʃ/ | sh |
| MEASURE, BEIGE | [ʒ] | /ʒ/ | zh |
| HOT, AHEAD | [h] | /h/ | h |
| CHIP, INCHES, ARCH | [ʧ] | /ʧ/ | ch |
| JUMP, AGES, JUDGE | [dʒ] | /dʒ/ | j |
| WHY, AWHILE | [hw] | /hw/ | hw |
| ONE, AWAY | [w] | /w/ | w |
| YES, ONION | [j] | /y/ | y |
| LIGHT, ALONE, TELL | [l] | /l/ | l |
| RUN, AROUND | [r] | /r/ | r |
| MAN, AMOUNT, SAME | [m] | /m/ | m |
| KNOW, LAND, SON | [n] | /n/ | n |
| SINGER, BRING | [ŋ] | /ŋ/ | ng |

13

other. For example, the word "I" is actually a diphthong. It is a combination of the two vowels, "ah" and "ee."

## CONSONANTS

Consonant sounds differ from vowels and diphthongs in that most of them are produced by blocking or restricting the air stream in some manner. The sound of the letter "p", for example, is made by blocking the breath stream with the lips, building up pressure inside the mouth, and then letting it explode by quickly separating the lips. Other phonemes, like the one represented by the letters "sh", cause the air to be squeezed between the tongue and the palate, making a hissing sound. Some consonant phonemes, such as "l" and "w," are produced by making relatively large movements of the articulators from one position to another.

## WRITING SOUNDS

By looking at Chart 2.1, you may have noticed that the vowel and diphthong symbols differ among the three alphabets presented somewhat more than do the consonants. To avoid any misunderstanding, therefore, the following pattern of writing sounds in this text will be observed:
1. When significant differences exsist between the phonetic and diacritic symbols, all three systems will be shown. For example, the sound of the word "I" will be shown as [aɪ]-/aɪ/-⟨ī⟩.
2. When both phonetic and diacritic symbols are the same except for brackets or parentheses, only the phonetic representation will be used. For example, the sound of the letter "p" is will be shown as [p].

## SUMMARY

The small number of letters in the alphabet (26) is not enough for the number of phonemes in English. For that reason, it has been necessary to develop systems of symbols to represent all of the sounds.
The phonemes of American English are divided into three groups: vowels, diphthongs, and consonants. Studying and practicing their production will improve your speaking ability in English.

# CHAPTER 3

# STRESS AND INTONATION

Two characteristics of American English which cause its learners problems are <u>stress</u> and <u>intonation</u>. These are needed to pronounce words correctly and to give interest and meaning to sentences. Stress relates to changes in the loudness of the voice. Intonation involves changes in its highness and lowness.

## THE CHARACTERISTIC OF STRESS IN SPEECH

Stress, in speech, involves the changing of loudness of words, or parts of words. Essentially, there are two main types of stress: <u>word stress</u> and <u>sentence stress</u>.

## WORD STRESS

Each English word is made up of one or more phonemes (see Chapter 2). Some words have only one phoneme; others have many. You may have noticed that not all sounds in all words are made equally loudly. In a word with several phonemes, some are produced louder than others.

<u>Syllables</u> are the smallest pronounceable parts of words. A few syllables have only one phoneme, but most contain several. Many words have only one syllable. Others contain two or more.

Consider the word "teacher." It has four different phonemes: [t]-(t), [i]-⟨ē⟩, [tʃ]-(ch), and [əʴ]-(ər). They are divided into two syllables: [titʃ]-(tēch) and [əʴ]-(ər).

If you look up "teacher" in a dictionary, you will find something like this: "teacher ['titʃəʴ]," or "teacher (tē'chər)." On the left is the word as it is normally spelled. Its pronunciation is on the right. The pronunciation of the first one is written in phonetics; the second in diacritics.

A stress mark (') is placed to the left of the "[t]" in the phonetic system. In the diacritic system used, it is to the right of the "(ē)" symbol. In both cases, it indicates that the first syllable, "['titʃ] or (tēch')" is to be spoken louder than the second, "[əʴ] or (ər)." We pronounce the word: "**teach** er", not "teach **er.**"

Not all dictionaries mark stress in the same way. Look up "teacher" in your dictionary. The stress mark may be before "teach" or after it. "Teach" may be printed with heavier type than "er." The mark may be to the right of the letter "e" in "teach". Whatever system your dictionary uses to indicate word stress, learn it now. It will help you in your study of the individual phonemes and in pronouncing the words that contain them.

Most two syllable words are stressed on the first syllable but many are stressed on the second. Consider the lists on the following page. You will find groups of two to five syllable words. Read each one aloud in order to experience the number of syllables and stress pattern each word has.

These words are written with their normal spelling. Word stress is indicated with bold type. Syllable divisions are indicated by blank spaces. The word: "tomorrow" would be written: "to **mor** row."

Some words have two stressed syllables: the main or primary stress and the less important or secondary stress. For example, the word "basketball" is stressed in this manner: "['bæskɪt,bɔl] (băs'kĭt-bôl')." In phonetic writing, the secondary

16

stress mark is placed to the left and below its syllable. In the AHD system, a light mark is placed to its right of the syllable with secondary stress.

In the practice material below stress is shown by bold type; secondary stress is shown with underlining; unstressed syllables have no marking; and all syllables are separated by a space.

## WORD STRESS PRACTICE

### TWO SYLLABLE WORDS - FIRST SYLLABLE STRESSED

| | | | |
|---|---|---|---|
| **an** swer | **good** ness | **o** pen | **test** <u>tube</u> |
| **ap** ple | **kit** chen | **pow** er | **un** der |
| **class** <u>room</u> | **let** ter | **res** ting | **vi** sit |
| **din** ner | **mo** ther | **sal** ty | **win** ter |
| **for** ty | **ne** ver | **su** gar | **ze** ro |

### TWO SYLLABLE WORDS - SECOND SYLLABLE STRESSED

| | | | |
|---|---|---|---|
| a **bout** | fif **teen** | per **cent** | sur **vive** |
| be **long** | ga **rage** | pre **tend** | to **day** |
| com **mand** | Ja **pan** | re **train** | to **night** |
| de **ny** | mis **take** | re **turn** | un **less** |
| e **quip** | o **bey** | sug **gest** | up **set** |

### THREE SYLLABLE WORDS - VARIOUS STRESSES

| | | | |
|---|---|---|---|
| **bat** te ry | O re <u>gon</u> | Ne **va** da | <u>dis</u> con **tent** |
| **ca** len dar | **se** na <u>tor</u> | re **la** ted | <u>quar</u> an **te** |
| **des** ti ny | com **pu** ter | re **mov** al | <u>Ja</u> pa **nese** |
| **fa** vo rate | de **po** sit | to **mor** row | <u>re</u> ap **pear** |
| **his** to ry | ga **ra** ges | <u>co</u> in **cide** | <u>re</u> u **nite** |

### FOUR AND FIVE SYLLABLE WORDS - VARIOUS STRESSES

| | | |
|---|---|---|
| <u>ac</u> ti **va** tion | **in** ter est ing | <u>me</u> tro **po** li tan |
| **com** pli <u>ca</u> ted | ki **lo** <u>me</u> ter | **na** tion a <u>li</u> sm |
| de **ve** lop ment | <u>li</u> ber **ta** ri an | <u>po</u> pu **la** tion |
| <u>e</u> co **no** mi cal | **li** ter a cy | ro **man** ti <u>ci</u> sm |
| <u>in</u> for **ma** tion | <u>me</u> di **oc** ri ty | <u>u</u> ni **ver** sal |

17

## SENTENCE STRESS

You have been examining words and the ways they are stressed. Some have only one syllable to stress, while others have two. When words are grouped together properly, they form phrases and sentences. In words, we stress syllables. In phrases and sentences we stress words.

Sometimes, we wish to stress only one word in a phrase or sentence. Often it is necessary to stress more than one. Occasionally, all words are stressed equally.

Consider the following example: "Jo needs a new car." Which words should be stressed, and which should not?

In most cases, the following types of words receive stress in phrases and sentences: subjects, objects, nouns, main verbs, adjectives, and adverbs. As a rule, all other types of words are unstressed. Pronouns may be stressed, when they are the subject or the object of the sentence.

In order to examine several sentences, we need to identify their words easily. We will use the following code for that purpose: S = the subject, O = the object, N = a noun, MV = the main verb, adj = an adjective, adv = an adverb, and P = a pronoun. Now let us look at our example again: "Jo(S-N) needs(MV) a new(adj) car(O-N)." If we indicate stressed words by underlining them and stress this sentence according to the ideas above, we would say:

<u>Jo</u> <u>needs</u> a <u>new</u> <u>car</u>.

If we read the sentence as it now looks, it would sound uninteresting. Usually, we place more stress on at least one word which we feel is most important in each sentence. Let us choose the word "new".

<u>Jo</u> <u>needs</u> a **NEW** <u>car</u>.

Note the way the sentence is written. "New" is printed in bold capital letters. "Jo," "needs," and "car" are all written in lower case letters and are

18

underlined. The word "a" is not underlined, indicating that it is unstressed. It is spoken softly.

Let us look at another example: "I have an exam tomorrow." If we code it, the sentence will look like this: "I(S-P) have(MV) an exam(O-N) tomorrow(adv)." If we decide that the important word is "exam," the sentence might be spoken like this:

I <u>have</u> an ex**AM** t<u>omorrow</u>.

Note that both "exam" and "tomorrow" have stressed and unstressed syllables. They are printed so as to demonstrate that the stressed syllable is spoken loudest.

## THE CHARACTERISTIC OF INTONATION IN SPEECH

Words and syllables are emphasized by changing more than just loudness. We also change <u>intonation</u> (the highness and lowness of the voice). Most of the time, our voice goes up when we say stressed syllables and/or words. We raise it highest on important words in phrases or sentences. Let us consider the first sentence again. If each stressed word is higher than the unstressed words, and the most stressed word is highest of all, it would look like this:

**NEW**

<u>Jo</u> <u>needs</u>          <u>car</u>.

a

Note that the word "new" is printed in bold type and placed higher than the other words. This indicates that it should be produced both louder and higher than the rest. Notice also that "a," the unstressed word, is placed lowest and, therefore, is produced softest and lowest.

## STRESS AND INTONATION IN STATEMENTS

The typical American English statement often ends with a downward intonation, that is, the pitch often lowers at the end of a sentence. Now look:

19

                          **NEW** <u>c</u>
        <u>Jo</u> <u>needs</u>           <u>a</u>
                   a              <u>r</u>.

        Let us consider the second sentence.  Including
markings   for   stress   and   intonation,  it might look
like this:

                          **AM**
              <u>have</u>      x      <u>mo</u>
        <u>I</u>            <u>e</u>
                   an         to    r
                                    row.

        The two   sentences   we ˙ have ̇ been   studying   have
demonstrated   typical   intonation and stress patterns
for statements.

## STRESS AND INTONATION IN QUESTIONS

        Questions generally fall into two classes:  those
that   demand   a   "yes"  or  "no"  answer and those which
require   an   explanation.   The   "yes-no"   questions
generally end with a rising intonation, that is, with
the voice at its highest at the end of the  sentence.
Others  types of questions are most often spoken like
statements.

        Let us look at this "yes-no" question:  "Did  you
pass   the   last   test?"   First   we   need   to code the
sentence:   "Did   you(S-P)   pass(MV)    the    last(adj)
test(O-N)?" If the most important word is "test," the
question would look like this:

                                    **ST?**
                                     **E**
              <u>you</u> <u>pass</u>        <u>last</u> **T**
        Did              the

        Note the rising intonation on  the   word   "test".
If   you   ask   such a question and receive the answer:
"Yes," you would probably follow it with  a  question
requiring   more information in the answer.   You might
ask: "What was your grade?" The coded sentence  would
look  like this: "What(O-P) was(MV) your grade(S-N)?"
With "grade" as the most important word, the sentence
would look like this:

20

GR
What was your A
DE?

Note that this pattern is very much like that of the statements above, with the intonation on the word "grade" going down.

## STRESS AND INTONATION PRACTICE

Following are examples of different types of sentences for your stress and intonation practice. You will find a few statements, examples of both types of questions and a simple conversation.

### STATEMENTS

C
Mis Kim go LA
ter is ing to S
S.
Mister Kim is going to class.

VE
sub h
His jects are ry a
rd.
His subjects are very hard.

QUITE
day h
To it is o
t.
Today it is quite hot.

B
Let's go E
to the A
CH.
Let's go to the beach.

GOOD
o
It is a n
e.
It is a good one.

LIKES
th
He e
m.
He likes them.

S
like W
I to I
M.
I like to swim.

GOOD de
That's i
a
a.
That's a good idea.

Yes-No Questions                    Regular Questions

```
                    geles?                                    LI
          like    AN                  Where do you   V
Do you         Los                                     E?
                                      Where do you live?
Do you like Los Angeles?
```

```
                    dent?                                   S
       you    GOOD stu                When do you   TU
Are       a                                           dy?
                                      When do you study?
Are you a good student?
```

Conversation - Person #1            Person #2

```
      MOR                                    YOU,
        n                                           to
Good      i                           How are      da
        ng.                                          y?
Good morning.                         How are you, today?
```

```
                  Y                      WELL,
I'm FI              O                  I'm      th
      N     How are                             an
      E.              U?                          ks.
I'm fine.  How are you?                I'm well, thanks.
```

```
              GO                                  L
Where     you   i                        go      U
      are         ng?                 I'm   ing to   N
Where are you going?                              CH.
                                      I'm going to lunch.
```

```
            U?                                 F
   I go      O                        That      U
May    with Y                              will be
                                                N.
May I go with you?                    That will be fun.
```

SUMMARY

    Stress and intonation are important factors in
developing your speaking skills. Imitate the stress
and intonation patterns you hear from good English
speakers. Use your cassette recorder constantly.

# CHAPTER 4

# VOWEL SOUNDS

In Standard American English, there are twelve distinct vowel phonemes. Each is produced by moving the speech organs in a particular way. Each has its own mouth opening, tongue position and lip shape. Figures 4.1 and 4.2 illustrate the movements needed to say the phonemes [ɑ]–/a/–(ä-ŏ) and [i]–/iʸ/–(ē).

FIGURE 4.1
[ɑ]–/a/–(ä-ŏ)

FIGURE 4.2
[i]–/iʸ/–(ē)

## PRODUCING A VOWEL SOUND

To produce the phoneme [ɑ]–/a/–(ä-ŏ), Figure 4.1, place your tongue nearly flat in the bottom of the mouth with its back rising slightly. Open your mouth fairly widely. To say [i]–/iʸ/–(ē), Figure 4.2, put the front of the tongue high toward the front of the mouth, with the mouth nearly closed. The arrow indicates that you should then move the tongue slightly upward as you close the jaw a little more. You may feel the jaw and tongue muscles tense slightly as the tongue moves closer to the palate. Both drawings have a star (*) in the position of the larynx, indicating that you should phonate when making them. Both sounds are voiced. Drawings and descriptions for the rest of the vowels appear on the practice pages (28-51).

Figure 4.3 illustrates the result of combining all of the vowel tongue positions into one drawing. If you look closely, you will note that the sounds can be grouped by the areas of the mouth in which they are produced. Some have the tongue highest in the front, some in the center and some in the back. By drawing lines dividing these areas, a chart can be created to help in making and discussing the vowels (Figure 4.4).

## THE VOWEL CHART

Based on the information above, the vowels can be placed on a vowel chart (Chart 4.1). Each of the areas on the chart is labled according to its relation to its position in the mouth. The lower left area, for example, represents the lower section of the front of the mouth. Similarly, the upper right area is the section which is high in the back of the mouth.

A particular vowel is placed on the chart because of the position of the tongue when the sound is produced. For example, when we say [i]−/i·/−⟨ē⟩, the highest part of the tongue is in the area which is high in the front of the mouth. The sound is called, therefore, a <u>high front vowel</u>. The [ɑ]−/a/−⟨ä−ŏ⟩ sound is made with the highest part of the tongue low in the back of the mouth. For that reason, it is a <u>low back vowel</u>.

Dividing each of the areas horizontally is a dotted line. You see one under the [i]−/i·/−⟨ē⟩ sound. As you remember, you must raise and tense your tongue slightly as you make the phoneme [i]−/i·/−⟨ē⟩. All vowels lying above the dotted lines do the same thing: the tongue muscles tighten and the tongue moves slightly as the sound is made. All together, there are six such vowels. They are

24

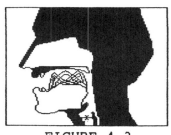

FIGURE 4.3
ALL VOWELS

FIGURE 4.4
VOWEL POSITIONS

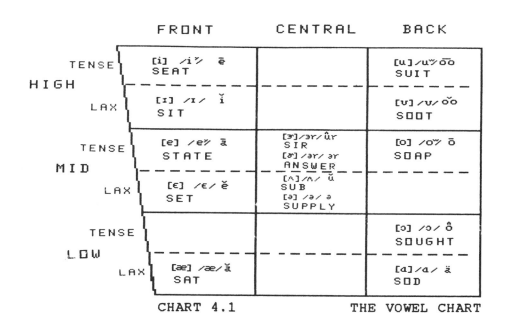

| | | FRONT | CENTRAL | BACK |
|---|---|---|---|---|
| HIGH | TENSE | [i] /i⁄ ē SEAT | | [u] /u⁄o͞o SUIT |
| | LAX | [ɪ] /ɪ/ ĭ SIT | | [ʋ] /ʋ/ o͝o SOOT |
| MID | TENSE | [e] /e⁄ ā STATE | [ɝ]/ər/ûr SIR [ɚ] /ər/ ər ANSWER | [o] /o⁄ ō SOAP |
| | LAX | [ɛ] /ɛ/ ĕ SET | [ʌ]/ʌ/ ŭ SUB [ə] /ə/ ə SUPPLY | |
| LOW | TENSE | | | [ɔ] /ɔ/ ô SOUGHT |
| | LAX | [æ] /æ/ ă SAT | | [ɑ]/ɑ/ ä SOD |

CHART 4.1                    THE VOWEL CHART

25

called <u>tense vowels</u>. The rest of the vowel phonemes, because they require no movement of the tongue while being produced, are called <u>lax vowels</u>. The complete descriptive name of the [i]–/i⸝/–⟨ē⟩ sound, therefore, a <u>high-front tense</u> vowel. The [ɑ]–/ɑ/–⟨ä–ŏ⟩ is a <u>low-back lax vowel</u>.

## MOUTH OPENINGS

The vowel chart provides information about the width of the mouth opening for each of the vowel sounds. The chart is divided into high, mid and low areas. In general, the mouth is nearly closed for the high vowels, about half open for the mid ones and nearly wide open for the low vowels.

## JAW MOVEMENTS

The jaw moves slightly during the production of the tense vowels (those above the dotted line). Such changes in position, and the direction of movement, are indicated by small arrows drawn on the lower jaw in the various illustrations. The jaw makes little or no movement for the lax vowels (those below the dotted line).

## LIP SHAPES

The shape of the lips is also indicated by the vowel chart. In general, the lips are spread, as in a smile, for the front vowels and rounded for the back ones. The lower the tongue position is for front vowels, the less spread the lips become. Similarly, the lower the tongue is for a back vowel, the less the lips will be rounded. The lips are neutral for the mid-central lax vowel, but for the mid-central tense phoneme, the edges of the lips may be pushed somewhat forward.

## USING THE VOWEL CHART

Each vowel has its own particular tongue position, mouth opening and lip shape. Some of them, the tense vowels, require movements of the jaw and tongue. The exact position and action of each vowel may be likened to the center of a target. When you attempt to make a sound that is new to you, you "aim"

26

your articulators toward the phoneme's position, just as a shooter does when aiming a rifle at a target. If you produce the phoneme correctly, you have "hit the mark," just as the shooter does when hitting the "bull's-eye" (the target center).

The vowel chart is quite useful, therefore, in demonstrating the position and action of the speech organs in producing the "target sounds." Learn the location of each vowel on the chart and its associated description. Fixing them in your mind will be of great help in hitting these vowel targets accurately.

## THE UNSTRESSED PHONEMES

Two of the phonemes presented on the chart are not represented in the practice pages. They are the sounds:[ɚ]-/ɚr/-⟨ər⟩ and [ə]-/ə/-⟨ə⟩. These two phonemes only appear in unstressed syllables of words (see Chapter 3). For all practical purposes, they are produced in the same manner as the stressed phonemes [ɝ]-/ɝr/-⟨ûr⟩ and [ʌ]-/ʌ/-⟨ŭ⟩. Though there is no formal practice for these sounds, you will have many opportunities to use them in the unstressed syllables and words in practice four of each lesson.

## THE PRACTICE PAGES

On the following pages, you will find practice material for each of the vowel phonemes. The same pattern will also be followed for the diphthongs (Chapter 5) and Consonants (Chapter 6). The first page for each sound contains its illustrations and description. A section indicating the various ways each phoneme can be spelled is then presented, followed by a listing of some of the problems which non-native speakers frequently have with the target sound. The facing page has several types of practice for the target sound.

27

THE VOWEL SOUND [i]—∕i∾∕—⟨ē⟩

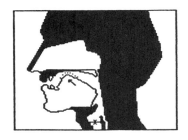
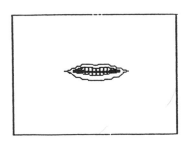

## DESCRIPTION

The phoneme [i]—∕i∾∕—⟨ē⟩ is the high-front tense vowel sound.  It is produced in the following manner:
1.  The front of the tongue is raised toward the front palate.
2.  The mouth is nearly closed.
3.  The lips are somewhat spread.
4.  Air is exhaled through the closed vocal folds, causing phonation.
5.  The tongue is raised further toward the palate as the jaw is raised slightly, resulting in a change in the sound.
6.  A slight increase in the tension of the tongue and jaw can be felt.

## SPELLINGS

The [i]—∕i∾∕—⟨ē⟩ sound is spelled in many ways: sound:

| | |
|---|---|
| "e" as in "evening" | "ei" as in "receive" |
| "ea" as in "speak" | "eo" as in "people" |
| "ee" as in "seem" | "ie" as in "believe" |

"y" as in "city"

## PROBLEMS

The most frequent problem with the [i]—∕i∾∕—⟨ē⟩ sound is that of substitution with the lax phoneme [ɪ]—∕ɪ∕—⟨ĭ⟩ so that "each" sounds like "itch," or "cheek" sounds like "chick."  When the [i]—∕i∾∕—⟨ē⟩ is in the final position of a word, it is incorrectly not tensed.  It is made like the phoneme [ɪ]—∕ɪ∕—⟨ĭ⟩, and appears to be incomplete.

[i]                              /iʸ/                                    ē

## PRACTICE A - WORDS

| | | | | | |
|---|---|---|---|---|---|
| EAch | EIther | betwEEn | nEEd | bE | sEE |
| EAger | Equal | complEte | pEOple | hE | shE |
| EAst | Even | fEEt | rEAd | manY | thrEE |
| EAsy | Evening | kEEp | sEEm | mE | verY |
| EAt | Evil | mEAns | thEse | onlY | wE |

## PRACTICE B - CONTRASTS

| | | | |
|---|---|---|---|
| EAch-itch | dEEp-dip | hE's-his | sEEn-sin |
| EAse-is | fEEl-fill | lEAve-live | shEEp-ship |
| EAt-it | fEEt-fit | pEAch-pitch | slEEp-slip |
| EEl-ill | grEEn-grin | rEAch-rich | shE'll-shill |
| bEAn-been | hEAt-hit | sEEk-sick | wE'll-will |

## PRACTICE C - SENTENCE CONTRASTS

1. EAch has an itch.
2. Please EAt it here.
3. He did the dEEd.
4. HE's at his house.
5. Pitch a pEAch.
6. Don't sit in that sEAt.
7. The shoes fit my fEEt.
8. ShE'll be a shill.
9. Tim is on a tEAm.
10. WE'll write a will.

## PRACTICE D - SENTENCES

1. Each of us needs to speak well.
2. Good breathing is needed for good speech.
3. To breathe, we need to think of three rules.
4. We don't need to breathe deeply for speech.
5. We need to breathe abdominally.
6. We breathe sufficiently to meet our need.
7. Speech breathing should be done frequently.
8. Short quick breathing is better then deep.
9. Breathing shallowly decreases speaking air.
10. Some people need a good breathing teacher.

### TONGUE TWISTER

Pete picks peaches
on Peach Tree Street
each evening.
"An evening picked
peach is sweetest,"
says picker Pete.

### LIMERICK

Says a cop named Steve Lundeen,
The best food to eat is a bean.
They're tasty and neat,
And not very sweet.
Green beans keep Steve lean.

## THE VOWEL SOUND [ɪ]–/ɪ/–(ĭ)

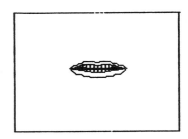

### DESCRIPTION

The phoneme [ɪ]–/ɪ/–(ĭ) is the high-front lax vowel sound. It is produced in the following manner:
1. The front of the tongue is raised toward the front palate.
2. The mouth is nearly closed.
3. The lips are slightly spread.
4. Air is exhaled through the closed vocal folds, causing phonation.

### SPELLINGS

The following spellings result in the [ɪ]–/ɪ/–(ĭ) sound:

"e" as in "English"
"ee" as in "been"
"ei" as in "surfeit"
"i" as in "ship"
"o" as in "women"
"u" as in "busy"
"ui" as in "building"
"y" as in "hymn"

### PROBLEMS

The most frequent problem with the phoneme [ɪ]–/ɪ/–(ĭ) is that of substitution. Often the [i]–/iʸ/–(ē) is heard so that "it" sounds like "eat," or "sit" sounds like "seat." Another, but less frequent substitution is the phoneme [ɛ]–/ɛ/–(ĕ) so that "ill" sounds like "ell," or "chick" sounds like "check."

[ɪ]                      /ɪ/                           ĭ

## PRACTICE A - WORDS

| English | Instrument | bEEn | dId | lIttle | thIs |
| If | Interest | begIn | fInish | mIddle | wIll |
| In | Interesting | bIll | gIve | pIck | wIndow |
| Inches | Is | bUIld | hIm | sImple | wInter |
| Indicate | It | cIty | hIs | sIt | wIsh |

## PRACTICE B - CONTRASTS

| Itch-each | hIll-heal | bIll-bell | pIn-pen |
| Is-ease | knIt-neat | dId-dead | pIt-pet |
| It-eat | lIve-leave | dIsk-desk | rId-red |
| bIn-bean | sIt-seat | lIt-let | sIt-set |
| dId-deed | shIp-sheep | mIt-met | wrIst-rest |

## PRACTICE C - SENTENCE CONTRASTS

1.  Eat It for lunch.
2.  Each dog has an Itch.
3.  The dean heard a dIn.
4   Please pItch a peach.
5.  TIm is on the team.
6.  The kIds wear Keds.
7.  LIft the left one.
8.  Get rId of a red one.
9.  Get ten bits of tIn.
10. I must rest my wrIst.

## PRACTICE D - SENTENCES

1.  The Mississippi River  is interesting  to visit.
2.  It is one of the biggest rivers in existence.
3.  This river begins in Minnesota.
4.  It rims Wisconsin, Illinois, and Missouri.
5.  Big cities exist beside the river.
6.  Minneapolis, Quincy, and Greenville are a few.
7.  Its banks are rich with history.
8.  Civil war ships battled at Vicksburg.
9.  International shipping is its biggest business.
10. The river is important in our economy.

### TONGUE TWISTER

The image in the
picture of my sister
is twisted.  Who will
untwist it so that
the image will be an
untwisted sister?

### LIMERICK

Lizzy Smith often gets dizzy
Whenever  she is very busy.
When things just don't click,
Her brain, it gets sick.
This miss is a real dizzy
    Lizzy.

31

THE VOWEL SOUND [e]—/eʸ/—⟨ā⟩

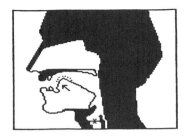
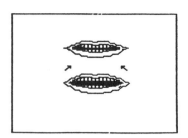

## DESCRIPTION

The phoneme [e]—/eʸ/—⟨ā⟩ is the mid-front tense vowel sound. It is produced in the following manner:
1. The front of the tongue is raised half way toward front palate.
2. The mouth is half open.
3. The lips are slightly spread.
4. Air is exhaled through the closed vocal folds, causing phonation.
5. As the sound is uttered, the jaw closes slightly, the lips become more spread, and the front of the tongue moves closer to the front palate, toward toward the position for the phoneme [i]—/iʸ/—⟨ē⟩.

## SPELLINGS

The [e]—/eʸ/—⟨ā⟩ sound can be spelled in the following ways:

"a" as in "state"          "ay" as in "play"
"ai" as in "wait"          "aye" as in "Faye"
"ao" as in "gaol"          "ea" as in "steak"
"au" as in "gauge"         "ei" as in "veil"
            "ey" as in "they"

## PROBLEMS

The primary problem with the [e]—/eʸ/—⟨ā⟩ sound is substitution. [ɛ]—/ɛ/—⟨ě⟩ may replace it so that "date" sounds like "debt," or "late" sounds like "let." Less frequently, [æ]—/æ/—⟨ă⟩ may be used, so that "take" sounds like "tack," or "steak" like "stack." [ɪ]—/ɪ/—⟨ĭ⟩ may also intrude so that "makes" sounds like "mix."

[e]　　　　　　　　/eʸ/　　　　　　　　ā

## PRACTICE A - WORDS

| | | | | | |
|---|---|---|---|---|---|
| Able | Ate | cAme | nAme | dAY | sAY |
| Age | EIGHt | chAnge | pAge | lAY | stAY |
| AId 帮助 | EIGHteen | grEAt | plAce | mAY | thEY |
| AIm 羊瞄准 | EIGHth | mAde | sAme | pAY | todAY |
| Asia | EIGHty | mAke | tAke | plAY | wAY |

## PRACTICE B - CONTRASTS

| | | | |
|---|---|---|---|
| Age-edge | lAte-let | Ate-at | sAve-salve |
| AId-Ed | rAke-wreck | AId-add | tAke-tack |
| dAte-debt | sAle-sell | cAme-cam | lAte-lit |
| gAte-get | trAde-tred | pAId-pad | mAkes-mix |
| lAId-led | wAIt-wet | plAne-plan | tAke-tick |

## PRACTICE C - SENTENCE CONTRASTS

1.  This lAce costs less.
2.  Let me be lAte.
3.  I met my mAte.
4.  RAId the red house.
5.  WAIt if you're wet.
6.  I Ate at home.
7.  Dan is a DAne.
8.  We ran in the rAIn.
9.  Don't brEAk the brick.
10. She Ate it.

## PRACTICE D - SENTENCES

1.  Waiting for late people is a plain pain.
2.  Lateness is hated behavior.
3.  It is stated that late people are hateful.
4.  Kate Lane is one who hates to wait.
5.  A man named Ray Gray had asked Kate for a date.
6.  Kate stated: "I'll wait for you by the gate.
7.  Ray was eighteen minutes late.
8.  The later Ray was, the more irate Kate became.
9.  When Ray came so late, Kate's anger was great.
10. Kate made Ray state he'd never be late again.

### TONGUE TWISTER

"The Navy is great,"
says Nate the sailor.
"Sailing freighters
over crazy waves
takes bravery,"
states sailor Nate.

### LIMERICK

A baseball player named James,
When hitting baseballs, aims
For the most distant gate
And, from home plate,
Hits home runs and wins many
games.

33

THE VOWEL SOUND [ɛ]–⁄ ɛ ⁄–⟨ĕ⟩

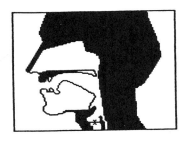
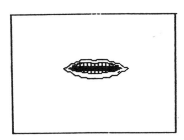

## DESCRIPTION

The phoneme [ɛ]–⁄ɛ⁄–⟨ĕ⟩ is the mid-front lax vowel sound. It is produced in the following manner:
1. The front of the tongue is raised half way toward front palate.
2. The mouth is half open.
3. The lips are slightly spread.
4. Air is exhaled through the lightly closed vocal folds, causing phonation.

## SPELLINGS

The [ɛ]–⁄ɛ⁄–⟨ĕ⟩ sound is spelled in the following ways:

"a" as in "many"          "ea" as in "breath"
"ai" as in "said"         "eo" as in "leopard"
"ay" as in "says"         "ie "as in "friend"
"e" as in "red"           "ue" as in "guest"

## PROBLEMS

The most frequent problem with the [ɛ]–⁄ɛ⁄–⟨ĕ⟩ sound is substitution. The [e]–⁄eʸ–⟨ā⟩ sound may be heard so that "red" sounds like "raid," or "met" like "mate." Frequently the [æ]–⁄æ⁄–⟨ă⟩ is used so that "bed" is pronounced like "bad," or "men" like "man." Often, the [ʌ]–⁄ʌ⁄–⟨ŭ⟩ is substituted so that "rest" sounds like "rust." The [ɪ]–⁄ɪ⁄–⟨ĭ⟩ is also heard so that "spell" sounds like "spill."

[ε]                    ╱ ε ╱                    ĕ

## PRACTICE A - WORDS

| | | | | | |
|---|---|---|---|---|---|
| Any | Else | Ever | agAIn | mEn | tEll |
| Anything | End | Every | gEt | sAId | vEry |
| Edge | Energy | Exercise | hElp | sEntence | wEll |
| Eggs | Engine | expEriment | lEtter | sEt | wEnt |
| Element | Enter | exprEss | mAny | spEll | whEn |

## PRACTICE B - CONTRASTS

| | | | |
|---|---|---|---|
| bEd-bid | tEll-till | pEn-pain | hEAd-had |
| dEAd-did | Edge-age | rEd-raid | sAId-sad |
| hEAd-hid | bEd-bayed | sEll-sail | sEnd-sand |
| nEck-nick | hEld-hailed | tEst-taste | tEn-ton |
| sEll-sill | mEn-main | bEd-bad | sEnd-sunned |

## PRACTICE C - SENTENCE CONTRASTS

1. Bid on the bEd.
2. SEll the sill to Ed.
3. Is Will wEll?
4. Buy tEn bits of tin.
5. Dane is in the dEn.
6. GEt a new gate.
7. The mace made a mEss.
8. TEll a tall tale.
9. That's a bad bEd.
10. Get a tEn ton truck.

## PRACTICE D - SENTENCES

1. Every student dreads taking tests.
2. Test taking, however, is very necessary.
3. Tests establish excellence in education.
4. Professors estimate grades with good tests.
5. When test day comes, students must be ready.
6. Lessons must have been read and digested.
7. Memory, not guess work, is the key to success.
8. The best test takers are rested before tests.
9. An educated guess is better than no answer.
10. A good breakfast gives one energy for testing.

### TONGUE TWISTER

Ten redheaded
beggars begged for
help.  When help
was rendered,
the beggars felt
better than ever.

### LIMERICK

The best bell seller, Red West,
Said his bells were the best.
He tested and tested
And none were bested.
They rang better than all the
    rest.

THE VOWEL SOUND [æ]—/æ/—⟨ă⟩

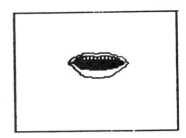

## DESCRIPTION

The phoneme [æ]—/æ/—⟨ă⟩ is the low-front lax vowel sound. It is produced in the following manner:
1. The front of the tongue is raised slightly toward front palate.
2. The mouth is nearly wide open.
3. The lips are slightly spread.
4. Air is exhaled through the lightly closed vocal folds, causing phonation.

## SPELLINGS

The [æ]—/æ/—⟨ă⟩ sound is spelled in only one way:

"a" as in "add"

## PROBLEMS

The most frequent problem with the phoneme [æ]—/æ/—⟨ă⟩ is that of substitution. Often, the [ɑ]—/ɑ/—⟨ä-ŏ⟩ is heard so that "can" sounds like "con," or "black" sounds like "block." Frequently, the [ɛ]—/ɛ/—⟨ĕ⟩ is used so that "man" is pronounced like "men," or "bad" like "bed." Also, the [ʌ]—/ʌ/—⟨ŭ⟩ is substituted so that "ran" sounds like "run."

36

[æ]                    / æ /                    ã

## PRACTICE A - WORDS

| | | | | | |
|---|---|---|---|---|---|
| Act | Alphabet | Answer | bAck | hAnd | mAd |
| Add | An | Apple | begAn | hAs | mAn |
| Adverb | And | As | cAn | hAve | plAn |
| After | Angle | At | exAmple | lAnd | rAn |
| Africa | Animal | Average | hAd | lAst | sAt |

## PRACTICE B - CONTRASTS

| | | | |
|---|---|---|---|
| Add-odd | mAd-mod | fAster-fester | bAd-bud |
| bAcks-box | sAck-sock | hAd-head | hAlf-huff |
| bAg-bog | sAd-sod | mAn-men | lAst-lust |
| cAt-cot | And-end | shAll-shell | mAd-mud |
| hAd-hod | bAd-bed | thAn-then | rAn-run |

## PRACTICE C - SENTENCE CONTRASTS

1. That's an odd Ad.
2. Don't botch a bAtch.
3. He hAd a hod.
4. The sot sAt here.
5. TAp it on the top.
6. That's a bAd bed.
7. I sAt on the set.
8. I shAll buy a shell.
9. Give me bAck the buck.
10. See that rAg rug.

## PRACTICE D - SENTENCES

1. Practically all on this planet want happiness.
2. Actually, happiness has a galaxy of meanings.
3. Happiness for the student is passing exams.
4. Parents are happy when their students pass, too.
5. Happiness for drivers is having no accidents.
6. A dancer is actually happiest when dancing.
7. The actor and actress are happy when acting.
8. Happiness doesn't happen by accident.
9. When plans don't "pan out", happiness is absent.
10. Planned happiness satisfies more than sadness.

### TONGUE TWISTER

Cats and rats make
bad companions.
Fast cats grab at
fat rats.  To have
fat cats, have many
fat rats.

### LIMERICK

Nancy, the dancer from France,
Wished to give acting a chance.
She put on her glasses
And took acting classes.
Now, Nancy can act, but not
    dance.

37

## THE VOWEL SOUND [ɑ]–/ɑ/–⟨ä-ŏ⟩

 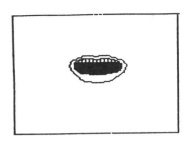

### DESCRIPTION

The phoneme [ɑ]–/ɑ/–⟨ä-ŏ⟩ is the low-back lax vowel sound. It is made in the following way:
1. The back of the tongue is raised slightly toward soft palate.
2. The mouth is nearly wide open.
3. The lips are in a neutral position.
4. Air is exhaled through the lightly closed vocal folds, causing phonation.

### SPELLINGS

The [ɑ]–/ɑ/–⟨ä-ŏ⟩ is spelled in the following ways:

> "a" as in "father"
> "ah" as in "ah"
> "ea" as in "heart"
> "o" as in "hot"

### PROBLEMS

The most frequent problem with the phoneme [ɑ]–/ɑ/–⟨ä-ŏ⟩ is that of substitution. Often, the [o]–/oʊ/–⟨ō⟩ is heard so that "sock" sounds like "soak," or "John" sounds like "Joan." Frequently, the [ʌ]–/ʌ/–⟨ŭ⟩ is used so that "cop" is pronounced like "cup," or "robber" like "rubber." Also, the [ɔ]–/ɔ/–⟨ô⟩ is substituted so that "cot" sounds like "caught." The [æ]–/æ/–⟨ă⟩ may be used so that "job" sounds like "jab."

38

[ɑ]                    /ɑ/                    ä, ŏ

## PRACTICE A - WORDS

| | | | | | |
|---|---|---|---|---|---|
| Ah | Odd | bOttom | fOllow | nOt | stOp |
| Object | Opera | cOnsonant | GOd | pOssible | tOp |
| Obvious | Operate | cOpy | gOt | prOblem | wAnt |
| Occupy | Opposite | dOllar | lOt | prOduct | wAsh |
| October | Oxygen | fAther | mOdern | rOck | wAtch |

## PRACTICE B - CONTRASTS

| | | | |
|---|---|---|---|
| blOck-bloke | wAnt-won't | sOck-suck | Odd-add |
| clOck-cloak | bOx-bucks | bOdy-bawdy | gOt-gat |
| cOp-cope | clOck-cluck | cOllar-caller | hOt-hat |
| gOt-goat | lOck-luck | cOt-caught | jOb-jab |
| nOt-note | nOt-nut | tOt-taught | nOt-gnat |

## PRACTICE C - SENTENCE CONTRASTS

1. The cOp can cope.
2. I got his goat.
3. That's nOt her note.
4  Don't rOb my robe.
5. The bum has a bOmb.
6. Put bucks in a bOx.
7. A pup drank some pOp.
8. I sawed the sOd.
9. The sOt sought help.
10. That add is quite Odd.

## PRACTICE D - SENTENCES

1. A doctor's job is not without problems.
2. A doctor has got to study a lot.
3. There are a lot of types of doctor.
4. Doctor John Roberts is a cardiologist.
5. His job is to stop heart problems.
6. One day, Doctor Roberts got a new patient.
7. Rhonda Lockwood had a blocked artery.
8. John had to operate on Rhonda's heart.
9. Doctor Robert's knowledge solved her problem.
10. Now, Rhonda is John Robert's "heart throb".

### TONGUE TWISTER

Do not put clocks in locked boxes. If a box is not locked, a clock is watched. A clock in a locked box is not watched.

### LIMERICK

A great crime stopper named Bob
Was the finest cop on the job.
He caught Tom, the bank robber,
And Tom, Bob did clobber.
In jail, Tom's not able to rob.

THE VOWEL SOUND [ɔ]-/ɔ/-⟨ô⟩

 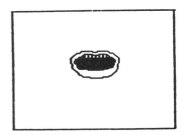

## DESCRIPTION

The phoneme [ɔ]-/ɔ/-⟨ô⟩ is the low-back tense vowel sound. It is produced in the following manner:
1. The back of the tongue is raised approximately half way toward the soft palate.
2. The mouth is nearly wide open.
3. The lips are very slightly rounded.
4. Air is exhaled through the lightly closed vocal folds, causing phonation.
5. As the phoneme is produced, the jaw is opened slightly wider, as tension increases in the jaw and tongue muscles.

## SPELLINGS

The [ɔ]-/ɔ/-⟨ô⟩ sound is spelled in the following ways:

| | |
|---|---|
| "a" as in "salt" | "aw" as in "law" |
| "ah" as in "Utah" | "augh" as in "caught" |
| "al" as in "walk" | "o" as in "long" |
| "au" as in "author" | "ough" as in "thought" |

## PROBLEMS

The most common problem with the sound [ɔ]-/ɔ/-⟨ô⟩ is that of substitution. Often, the [a]-/a/-⟨ä-ŏ⟩ is heard so that "awed" sounds like "odd," or "caught" sounds like "cot." Frequently, the [o]-/o/-⟨ō⟩ is used so that "called" is pronounced like "cold," or "jaw" like "Joe." Also, the [ʌ]-/ʌ/-⟨ŭ⟩ may be heard so that "boss" sounds like "bus," or "cough" sounds like "cuff."

40

[ɔ]                    /ɔ/                    ô

## PRACTICE A - WORDS

| All | Always | acrOss | dOg | sOft | drAW |
|-----|--------|--------|-----|------|------|
| Almost | AUthor | alOng | fAll | thOUGHt | jAW |
| Already | AUto | becAUse | gOne | wALked | lAW |
| Also | Off | cAlled | lOng | wAll | rAW |
| Although | Often | cAUse | smAll | wAter | sAW |

## PRACTICE B - CONTRASTS

| AWed-odd | hAWk-hock | bAll-bowl | bOss-bus |
|----------|-----------|-----------|----------|
| chALk-chock | sAWed-sod | bOUGHt-boat | bOUGHt-but |
| dAWn-don | tALk-tock | cOst-coast | cOst-cussed |
| cAller-collar | tAUGHt-tot | lAWn-loan | lAW-low |
| cAUGHt-cot | rAW-rah | sAWed-sewed | sAW-so |

## PRACTICE C - SENTENCE CONTRASTS

1. Don is up at dAWn.
2. Hock the hAWk, now.
3. Rah! It's rAW.
4. The tot was tAUGHt.
5. Joe broke his jAW.
6. Paul bOUGHt a boat.
7. A coat got cAUGHt.
8. My bOss rides the bus.
9. That gun is gOne.
10. That's the wrOng rung.

## PRACTICE D - SENTENCES

1. Almost all workers have bosses.
2. Bosses can be awfully bad or awfully good.
3. Paul Walker works in a law office.
4. Paul's boss, Saul, is a strong leader.
5. Saul called Paul into the office.
6. He wanted Paul to play golf on Saturday.
7. Paul thought: "I'm better at golf than Saul."
8. "If Saul loses at golf, he'll be awfully mad."
9. Paul played good golf, and beat Saul badly.
10. Paul was wrong; Saul, the boss, applauded Paul.

### TONGUE TWISTER

Maude, the long song singer sang the long song wrong. "Long songs ought not to be sung wrong," says song singer Maude.

### LIMERICK

A baseball player, so tall,
Caught balls hit to the wall.
His arm was so strong,
And his jumps were so long
No batter could "get on the ball."

41

THE VOWEL SOUND [o]—/o‿/—⟨ō⟩

 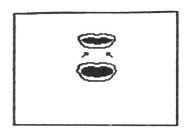

## DESCRIPTION

The phoneme [o]—/o‿/—⟨ō⟩ is the mid-back tense vowel sound. It is produced in the following manner:

1. The back of the tongue is raised mid way between the floor of the mouth and the soft palate.
2. The mouth is half open.
3. The lips are rounded.
4. Air is exhaled through the lightly closed vocal folds, causing phonation.
5. As the sound is produced, the tongue is raised toward the soft palate to the position for the sound [u]—/u‿/—⟨o͞o⟩, the mouth closes to the slightly open position, and the lips become more rounded.

## SPELLINGS

The [o]—/o‿/—⟨ō⟩ sound is spelled in these ways:

"au" as in "chauvanism"     "eau" as in "bureau"
"eo" as in "yeoman"         "ew" as in "sew"
"o" as in "cold"            "oa" as in "coat"
"oe" as in "foe"            "oo" as in "Van Loon"
"ough" as in "though"       "ow" as in "blow"
                "owe" as in "owe"

## PROBLEMS

The most frequent problem with the phoneme [o]—/o‿/—⟨ō⟩ is that of substitution. Often, the [ɔ]—/ɔ/—⟨ô⟩ is heard so that "own" sounds like "on," or "boat" sounds like "bought." The [ʌ]—/ʌ/—⟨ŭ⟩ may be used so that "wrote" sounds like "rut."

42

[o]                    /o͞o/                    ō

## PRACTICE A - WORDS

| | | | | | |
|---|---|---|---|---|---|
| OAk | Only | bOth | hOme | alsO | knOW |
| Ocean | Open | clOse | mOst | belOW | nO |
| Oh | Over | cOld | thOse | fOllOW | shOW |
| Ohio | OWn | dOn't | tOld | gO | slOW |
| Old | OWner | hOld | whOle | grOW | sO |

## PRACTICE B - CONTRASTS

| | | | |
|---|---|---|---|
| OWn-on | dOn't-daunt | JOE-jaw | hOme-hum |
| OWning-awning | hOld-hauled | lOW-law | knOWn-none |
| bOAt-bought | lOAn-lawn | rOW-raw | phOne-fun |
| bOWl-ball | phOne-fawn | sEW-saw | rOAst-rust |
| cOld-called | wrOte-wrought | sO-saw | wrOte-rut |

## PRACTICE C - SENTENCE CONTRASTS

1.  I'm on my OWn.
2.  I bought a bOAt.
3.  You bOWl with a ball.
4   Call about the cOAl.
5.  DOn't daunt anyone.
6.  JOE broke his jaw.
7.  I saw her sEW.
8.  The nut wrOte a nOte.
9.  It is fun to phOne.
10. It is sEWn in the sun.

## PRACTICE D - SENTENCES

1.  Joe and Joan wrote books about boats.
2.  Joan and Joe own an old oak sailboat.
3.  The oak boat is their only home.
4.  Joe and Joan rode their boat around the globe.
5.  They wrote the whole tale of their ocean voyage.
6.  They told of the cold days on the open ocean.
7.  They wrote of the hole in the boat's hold.
8.  Some days were slow; others seemed only moments.
9.  When the trip was over, it was time to go home.
10. Since home is an old boat, they're still afloat.

### TONGUE TWISTER

"Old ropes won't
hold new boats,"
the old boat owner
told hopeful new
boaters.  "New boats
need new ropes."

### LIMERICK

"I know," said old Mister Snow,
"The stock which high will go."
So we gave him our gold,
And were left in the cold.
Thanks to Snow, we have no gold
    to show.

## THE VOWEL SOUND [ʊ]-/ʊ/-⟨ŏŏ⟩

## DESCRIPTION

The phoneme [ʊ]-/ʊ/-⟨ŏŏ⟩ is the high-back lax vowel sound. It is produced in the following manner:
1.  The back of the tongue is raised high in the back of the mouth, toward the soft palate.
2.  The mouth is slightly open.
3.  The lips are slightly rounded.
4.  Air is exhaled through the lightly closed vocal folds, causing phonation.

## SPELLINGS

The [ʊ]-/ʊ/-⟨ŏŏ⟩ sound may be spelled in the following ways:

"o" as in "wolf"
"oo" as in "look"
"oul" as in "should"
"u" as in "push"

## PROBLEMS

The most frequent problem with the phoneme [ʊ]-/ʊ/-⟨ŏŏ⟩ is that of substitution. Often, the [u]-/u͞/-⟨ō͞o⟩ is heard so that "pull" sounds like "pool," or "look" sounds like "Luke." The phoneme [ʌ]-/ʌ/-⟨ŭ⟩ may be substituted so that "look" sounds like "luck," or "took" like "tuck." Less frequently, the [o]-/o͞/-⟨ō⟩ may be used so that "should" sounds like "showed".

[ʊ]                                        /ʊ/                                        ŏŏ

## PRACTICE A - WORDS

| bOOk  | cOOked   | gOOd   | pUll   | rOOf      | wOOd     |
|-------|----------|--------|--------|-----------|----------|
| bUll  | cOULd    | hOOd   | pUlled | shOULd    | wOOl     |
| brOOk | cOUldn't | hOOk   | pUsh   | shOULdn't | wOman    |
| bUsh  | fOOt     | lOOk   | pUshed | sUgar     | wOULd    |
| cOOk  | fUll     | lOOked | pUt    | tOOk      | wOUldn't |

## PRACTICE B - CONTRASTS

| cOULd-cooed | pUll-pool     | cOULd-cud | cOOk-Coke    |
|-------------|---------------|-----------|--------------|
| fUll-fool   | shOULd-shoed  | lOOk-luck | cOULd-code   |
| gOOd-gooed  | stOOd-stewed  | pUt-putt  | fUll-foal    |
| hOOd-who'd  | wOULd-wooed   | tOOk-tuck | gOOd-goad    |
| lOOk-Luke   | bOOk-buck     | bUll-bowl | stOOd-stowed |

## PRACTICE C - SENTENCE CONTRASTS

1.  It cOULd have cooed.
2.  The fool is too fUll.
3.  LOOk at Luke.
4   PUll her to the pool.
5.  Who'd buy that hOOd?
6.  The bOOk cost a buck.
7.  It cOULd chew its cud.
8.  I tOOk a tuck in it.
9.  The bUll broke a bowl.
10. COULd you code this?

## PRACTICE D - SENTENCES

1.  Brooke Goodman is a good wood worker.
2.  She can make wood cabinets as good as anyone.
3.  She loves the look and feel of good wood.
4.  Brooke is a wood carver and a good cook, too.
5.  Once, she took wood carving tools to the woods.
6.  She carried a well cooked lunch and a good book.
7.  At a brook, she ate her goods and read the book.
8.  A woodsman named Woods talked to Brooke.
9.  Woods saw that her cooking and looks were good.
10. Now its Brooke Woods who carves wood and cooks.

### TONGUE TWISTER

How much wood could
a woodchuck chuck if
a woodchuck could
chuck wood? Should
woodchucks chuck
wood if they could?

### LIMERICK

The very good cook in Chinook
Got a good looking cook book.
The  book was no good.
It looks like he should
Buy books that read better than
   look."

45

## THE VOWEL SOUND [u]-/u⁓-(ōō)

 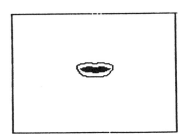

## DESCRIPTION

The phoneme [u]-/u⁓-(ōō) is the high-back tense vowel sound. It is produced in the following manner:
1. The back of the tongue is raised high in the back of the mouth, toward the soft palate.
2. The mouth is slightly open.
3. The lips are slightly rounded.
4. Air is exhaled through the lightly closed vocal folds, causing phonation.
5. As the sound is made, the mouth closes slightly, the lips become more rounded, and the back of the tongue moves closer to the soft palate.

## SPELLINGS

The [u]-/u⁓-(ōō) sound may be spelled in the following ways:

"au" as in "beauty"          "ou" as in "you"
"eu" as in "rheumatic"       "ough" as in "through"
"ew" as in "drew"            "u," [ju]-/yu⁓/-(yōō),
"ioux" as in "Sioux"              as in "use"
"o" as in "do"               "ue" as in "due"
"oe" as in "shoe"            "ui" as in "suit"
"oo" as in "food"            "wo" as in "two"

## PROBLEMS

The primary problem with the [u]-/u⁓-(ōō) is that of substitution. Often, the [ʊ]-/ʊ/-(ŏŏ) is heard so that "pool" sounds like "pull," or "Luke" sounds like "look."

46

[u]                              ⁄u⁚                              o͞o

## PRACTICE A - WORDS

| bEAUty | grOUp | schOOl | blUE | glUE | thrEW |
|--------|-------|--------|------|------|-------|
| chOOse | hUman | stUdent | continUE | knEW | trUE |
| cOOl | mOOn | Use | crEW | nEW | yOU |
| fOOd | mOve | Usually | dO | twO | valUE |
| frUIt | rOOm | whOse | fEW | thrOUGH | whO |

## PRACTICE B - CONTRASTS

cOOed-could          pOOl-pull
fOOl-full            shOEd-should
gOOed-good           stEWed-stood
kOOk-cook            whO'd-hood
LUke-look            wOOed-would

## PRACTICE C - SENTENCE CONTRASTS

1. It could have cOOed.        6. Pull it from the pOOl.
2. The fOOl is full.          7. I should've shOEd it.
3. Oh good! It's gOOed.       8. We stood and stEWed.
4. The kOOk can cook.         9. WhO'd want this hood?
5. Please look at LUke.      10. He would not be wOOed.

## PRACTICE D - SENTENCES

1. June Coolidge was born at the new moon one June.
2. June, therefore, makes June sing happy tunes.
3. June starts using her cool pool in June.
4. She buys new shoes when the June moon is full.
5. June usually takes a cruise to Peru, too.
6. On one June cruise, June met a blue-eyed sailor.
7. Blue-eyes thought June's eyes were beautiful.
8. The two knew that a new love was blooming.
9. Now June has a new reason to sing tunes in June.
10. One noon, last June, June and blue-eyes married.

### TONGUE TWISTER

Is soup more useful
than stew or is new
stew better fuel for
a cruising crew? You
must chew stew, but
use a spoon for soup.

### LIMERICK

A shoe seller in Newport News
Sells only beautiful shoes.
Buy his shoes, as a rule,
And you'll be no fool.
Newport News shoes are super
   to use.

47

## THE VOWEL SOUND [ɝ]-/ɝr/-(ûr)

### DESCRIPTION

The phoneme [ɝ]-/ɝr/-(ûr) is the mid-central tense vowel sound. It is made in the following way:
1. It begins with the tongue in either of two positions:
   A. With the tongue tip up, by the front palate, and its center raised near the center palate, or:
   B. With the tongue tip behind the lower front teeth, and its front and center near the central palate.
2. Air is exhaled through the lightly closed vocal folds, causing phonation.
3. The mouth is half open.
4. The lips are in a neutral position, but their outer edges may be pushed slightly forward.
5. As the sound is made, the jaw closes slightly and the tongue moves closer to the palate.

### SPELLINGS

The sound [ɝ]-/ɝr/-(ûr) may be spelled in the following ways:

"er" as in "verse"      "or" as in "work"
"ir" as in "bird"       "ur" as in "turn"

### PROBLEMS

The most common problem associated with the [ɝ]-/ɝr/-(ûr) phoneme is substitution, specifically with the sound [ʌ]-/ʌ/-(ŭ) so that "bird" sounds like "bud," or turn sounds like "ton." The [ɛr]-/ɛr/-(âr) may be used, so that "bird" sounds like "bared," or "fur" sounds like "fair."

48

[ɝ]                    /ɜr/                              ûr

## PRACTICE A - WORDS

| EARly      | URge     | cURve  | lEARn  | tURn   | fUR    |
|------------|----------|--------|--------|--------|--------|
| EARn       | bIRd     | fIRm   | nERve  | wORd   | hER    |
| EARned     | bIRth    | fIRst  | pERson | wORk   | preFER |
| EARth      | bURn     | gIRl   | sEARch | wORld  | sIR    |
| EARthquake | cERtain  | hEARd  | sERve  | wORth  | wERE   |

## PRACTICE B - CONTRASTS

| bERm-bum  | ERRed-aired   | blUR-blare |
|-----------|---------------|------------|
| bIRd-bud  | bIRd-bared    | cUR-care   |
| bURn-bun  | fURry-fairy   | fUR-fair   |
| fERn-fun  | hURry-hairy   | hER-hair   |
| tURn-ton  | MURry-merry   | pURR-pair  |

## PRACTICE C - SENTENCE CONTRASTS

1.  See a bum on a bERm.       6.  The bear got a bURR.
2.  The bIRd ate a bud.        7.  I care for the cURR.
3.  Don't bURn the bun.        8.  That's a fair fUR.
4   HURry up, Harry.           9.  She cut hER hair.
5.  MURry is merry.            10. Where is the whIRR?

## PRACTICE D - SENTENCES

1.  In today's world, students earn money to learn.
2.  Early or late, they work to earn and learn.
3.  They hurry to class and scurry to work.
4.  Most schools have an urgent need for workers.
5.  At first, they worry that enough will turn up.
6.  They worry in vain, for workers hurry to apply.
7.  The first person there usually gets the work.
8.  We often say: "the early bird gets the worm."
9.  Most workers serve colleges well as they learn.
10. Serving, working and learning are all important.

### TONGUE TWISTER

Thirty birds were
perched in a birch
tree.  All thirty
were early birds,
and yearned for
squirming worms.

### LIMERICK

A girl with a curl was learning
How to cook without burning.
She stirred and she stirred,
And said not a word.
Now the girl a cook's wage is
    earning.

## THE VOWEL SOUND [ʌ]–/ʌ/–⟨ŭ⟩

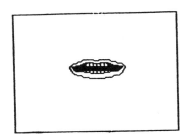

## DESCRIPTION

The phoneme [ʌ]–/ʌ/–⟨ŭ⟩ is the mid-central lax vowel sound. It is produced in the following manner:
1. The center of the tongue is raised half way toward the center of the palate.
2. The mouth is half open.
3. The lips are neutral.
4. Air is exhaled through the closed vocal folds, causing phonation.

## SPELLINGS

The [ʌ]–/ʌ/–⟨ŭ⟩ sound is spelled in these ways:

> "a" as in "was"
> "o" as in "come"
> "oe" as in "does"
> "oo" as in "blood"
> "ou" as in "touch"
> "u" as in much

## PROBLEMS

The [ʌ]–/ʌ/–⟨ŭ⟩ is produced with the position of the tongue close to that of the phonemes [ɑ]–/ɑ/–⟨ä-ŏ⟩, [ɔ]–/ɔ/–⟨ô⟩, [ʊ]–/ʊ/–⟨o͝o⟩, and [æ]–/æ/–⟨ă⟩. As a result, these sounds are commonly substituted for the [ʌ]–/ʌ/–⟨ŭ⟩, so that "cut" sounds like "cot," "dug" sounds like "dog," "tuck" sounds like "took," and "luck" sounds like "lack."

[ʌ]                    /ʌ/                           ŭ

## PRACTICE A - WORDS

| Of      | Uncle  | blOOd  | frOm   | One     | tOUch    |
|---------|--------|--------|--------|---------|----------|
| Other   | Up     | bUt    | fUn    | resUlt  | trOUble  |
| Oven    | Upper  | cOme   | jUmp   | sOme    | wAs      |
| Ugly    | Us     | dOEs   | mOney  | sOn     | wOn      |
| Under   | Utter  | enOUgh | mOnth  | sUn     | wOnder   |

## PRACTICE B - CONTRASTS

| bUs-bass  | cOme-calm | bUs-boss  | bUck-book  |
|-----------|-----------|-----------|------------|
| cUt-cat   | dUck-dock | dUg-dog   | cUd-could  |
| nUt-gnat  | lUck-lock | hUll-hall | lUck-look  |
| mUd-mad   | nUt-not   | gUlf-golf | pUtt-put   |
| rUg-rag   | rUb-rob   | lUng-long | tUck-took  |

## PRACTICE C - SENTENCE CONTRASTS

1.  He has a lack of lUck.
2.  Sam wants sOme.
3.  His boss rode the bUs.
4.  The song was sUng.
5.  Someone cUt the cot.
6.  Don is dOne.
7.  A dUck is on a dock.
8.  It is not a nUt.
9.  A book costs a bUck.
10. She took a tUck.

## PRACTICE D - SENTENCES

1.  Each one of us should love this country.
2.  Many of us come from other countries.
3.  Our mothers and brothers taught us to love them.
4.  Coming to a new country is tough.
5.  New customs must be studied.
6.  Another language must be uttered.
7.  Love for the new country is slow in coming.
8.  To discover such love is wonderful.
9.  Someone said that too much love is trouble.
10. My uncle says: "a country takes a lot of love."

### TONGUE TWISTER

A dozen ducks sat in
the sun.  One said
that the sun was fun.
Another said that mud
was fun.  "Mud and sun
are fun," said others.

### LIMERICK

My country cousin's son
Thinks running races is fun.
He bet me a buck
That he'd have good luck,
And he won, the son-of-a-gun.

## SUMMARY

In order to develop effective production of the vowel phonemes, a good understanding of their articulation is needed. Studying the vowel chart provides an effective way of learning the positions for the lips, tongue and jaw for each target sound. After that, the most effective way to get these sounds into you conversational speech is: PRACTICE!

# CHAPTER 5

# DIPHTHONG SOUNDS

There are three diphthong sounds in Standard American Speech. As previously mentioned, a diphthong is a combination of two vowels. More properly, a diphthong is a sound which results from the movement of the articulators from the position of one vowel to another. This is illustrated on the diphthong chart (Chart 5.1) and in the drawings on pages 56-60.

## DIPHTHONG PRODUCTION

To produce the [aɪ]-/aɪ/-⟨ī⟩, [ɔɪ]-/ɔɪ/-⟨oi⟩ and [aʊ]-/aʊ/-⟨ou⟩ sounds accurately, several coordinated actions are necessary. Diphthongs are all produced by closing the mouth and raising the tongue. The lips either become more spread or more rounded, depending upon the position of the second sound in the combination. The first sound (or element) in each diphthong is made louder than the second.

The most important characteristic of diphthongs is movement. From beginning to end, the articulators continually change position. The small arrows on the individual diagrams (pages 56, 58 and 60) indicate the direction of movement. For all three phonemes, the movement is upward, with the mouth closing and the tongue rising.

The most frequent error made in diphthong production is that of not finishing the sound. For example, should the lips not be appropriately rounded

small when compared with those of the three
diphthongs discussed in this chapter.

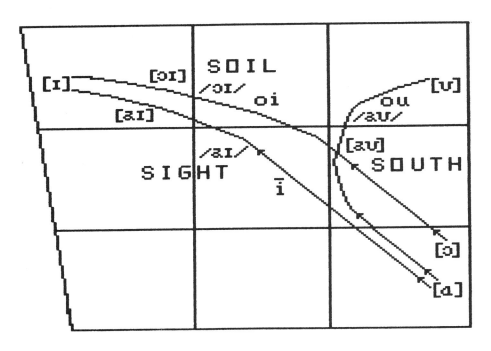

Chart 5.1 - DIPHTHONGS

or spread, the diphthongs will be distorted. If the articulator movement is incomplete, "time" may sound like "Tom," or "shout" like "shot."

## THE DIPHTHONG CHART

Each of the three diphthongs drawn on Chart 5.1 begins with the tongue in the low-back position. Two of them start with the phoneme [ɑ]–/ɑ/–⟨ä-ŏ⟩. The third begins with the vowel sound [ɔ]–/ɔ/–⟨ô⟩. For two of the diphthongs, the tongue rises to the high-front [ɪ]–/ɪ/–⟨ĭ⟩ position. One ends with the tongue at the location of the high-back vowel [ʊ]–/ʊ/–⟨o͝o⟩.

## PRACTICE

As you work on these sounds, do so slowly. They are longer than the vowels and diphthongs of most other languages. If you take your time in saying them, you will be able to make the adjustments in the movement of your articulators to produce them correctly.

55

## THE DIPHTHONG SOUND [aɪ]-/aɪ/-⟨ī⟩

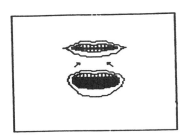

### DESCRIPTION

The phoneme [aɪ]-/aɪ/-⟨ī⟩ is the low-back to high-front diphthong sound. It is produced in the following manner:
1. The back of the tongue is raised slightly in the back of the mouth toward the soft palate.
2. The mouth is nearly wide open.
3. The lips are neutral.
4. Air is exhaled through the closed vocal folds, causing phonation.
5. As the sound is started, the jaw moves to the nearly closed position, the lips become spread and the front of the tongue moves close to the front palate, toward the [i]-/iˊ/-⟨ē⟩ position.

### SPELLINGS

The [aɪ]-/aɪ/-⟨ī⟩ sound is spelled in these ways:

| | |
|---|---|
| "ai" as in "aisle" | "igh" as in "sight" |
| "eigh" as in "height" | "is" as in "island" |
| "ey" as in "geyser" | "oi", [wai] as in "choir" |
| "eye" as in "eye" | "uy" as in "buy" |
| "i" as in "write" | "y" as in "try" |
| "ie" as in "ties" | "ye" as in "lye" |

### PROBLEMS

The most common problem with the phoneme [aɪ]-/aɪ/-⟨ī⟩ is incompleteness. Often, the sound's movements are not completed, so that "right" sounds like "rot," or "time" like "Tom." The [æ]-/æ/-⟨ă⟩ may be substituted, so that "fine" sounds like "fan". The [ɔɪ]-/ɔɪ/-⟨oi⟩ may be used, so that "line" sounds like "loin."

[aɪ]                    /aɪ/                    ī

## PRACTICE A - WORDS

| EYEs | IdentifY | drIve | lIne | bY | mY |
|------|----------|-------|------|-----|------|
| I | I'll | fInd | rIGHt | bUY | skY |
| Ice | Iron | kInd | tIme | dIE | supplY |
| I'd | ISland | lIGHt | whIle | hIGH | trY |
| Idea | Item | lIke | wrIte | lIE | whY |

## PRACTICE B - CONTRASTS

| kIte-cot | tIGHt-tot | bIke-back | sIGHed-sad |
|----------|-----------|-----------|------------|
| lIGHt-lot | tIme-Tom | fIne-fan | kInd-coined |
| nIGHt-not | wInd-wand | mIGHt-mat | lIar-lawyer |
| rIGHt-rot | I'd-add | rIGHt-rat | lIne-loin |
| sIGHt-sot | I'm-am | sIGHt-sat | tIE-toy |

## PRACTICE C - SENTENCE CONTRASTS

1. We've a lot of lIGHt.
2. It's not nIGHt, now.
3. What's the tIme, Tom.
4. Can you wInd a wand?
5. I'd add them, now.
6. That's a fIne fan.
7. He had to hIde.
8. I mIGHt buy a mat.
9. The boy will bUY it.
10. Lloyd lIEd about that.

## PRACTICE D - SENTENCES

1. Mike Smiley, the pieman, makes nice pies.
2. Mike's pies are always quite right.
3. Any pie of Mike's is quite delightful.
4. One night, Eileen came to buy some apple pie.
5. Eileen wanted a slice of pie with ice cream.
6. Mike didn't like to serve ice cream with pie.
7. "I'm griped by pie and ice cream," said Mike.
8. "Then I won't buy pie either," cried Eileen.
9. That night, Mike tried Eileen's idea.
10. For delightful pie and ice cream, try Mike's.

### TONGUE TWISTER

"Try my nice spices," says Ida, the nice spice pricer. "My spices are not as high priced as Mr. White's," cries Ida.

### LIMERICK

Trying to think of a rhyme
Isn't easy, all of the time.
Some words aren't right.
Some won't fit, quite.
The right ones make the bells
    chime.

57

## THE DIPHTHONG SOUND [ɔɪ]–/ɔɪ/–⟨oi⟩

 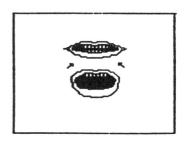

DESCRIPTION

The phoneme [ɔɪ]–/ɔɪ/–⟨oi⟩ is the low-back tense to high-front diphthong sound. It is produced in the following manner:
1.  The back of the tongue is raised somewhat in the back of the mouth toward the soft palate.
2.  The mouth is nearly wide open.
3.  The lips are slightly rounded.
4.  Air is exhaled through the closed vocal folds, causing phonation.
5.  As the sound is started, the jaw moves to the nearly closed position, the lips become slightly rounded and the front of the tongue moves close to the front palate, toward the position for the phoneme [i]–/iʸ/–⟨ē⟩.

SPELLINGS

The [ɔɪ]–/ɔɪ/–⟨oi⟩ sound may be spelled in these ways:

> "oi" as in "noise"
> "oy" as in "joy"
> "uoy" as in "buoy"

PROBLEMS

The most frequent difficulty with the diphthong [ɔɪ]–/ɔɪ/–⟨oi⟩ is incompleteness. Often, the sound's movements are not finished ,so that "boil" sounds like "ball," or "joy" like "jaw." The [aɪ]–/aɪ/–⟨ī⟩ sound may be substituted, so that "voice" sounds like "vice." More rarely, [o]–/oʷ/–⟨ō⟩ may be used, so that "toy" sounds like "toe." [aʊ]–/aʊ/–⟨ou⟩ is also noted, so that "boy" sounds like "bough."

[ɔɪ]                    /ɔɪ/                    oi

## PRACTICE A - WORDS

| | | | | | |
|---|---|---|---|---|---|
| OIl | bOIl | fOIl | pOInt | annOY | emplOY |
| OIlcloth | cOIl | jOIn | quOIts | anOInt | enjOY |
| OIlproof | cOIn | jOInt | sOIl | bOY | jOY |
| OIntment | enjOYed | mOIst | vOIce | bUOY | sOY |
| OYster | emplOYed | nOIse | vOYage | cOY | tOY |

## PRACTICE B - CONTRASTS

| | | | |
|---|---|---|---|
| OIl-all | jOY-jaw | vOIce-vice | OIl-owl |
| bOIled-bald | ROY-raw | tOY-tie | bOY-bough |
| cOIL-call | OIl-I'll | OIled-old | cOY-cOW |
| fOIl-fall | bOIl-bile | cOIn-cone | jOInts-jounce |
| nOIse-gnaws | fOIl-file | tOY-toe | pOInts-pounce |

## PRACTICE C - SENTENCE CONTRASTS

1. All OIl is high.
2. I won't bOIl a ball.
3. ROY likes raw fish.
4. The Isle has no OIL.
5. Never bOIl bile.
6. The cone costs a cOIn.
7. The tOY broke my toe.
8. I OIled the old car.
9. OIl fell on the owl.
10. The bOY broke a bough.

## PRACTICE D - SENTENCES

1. Boys enjoy making noise with toys.
2. Noisy boys often annoy their neighbors.
3. Roy was the noisiest boy of all.
4. Roy's voice was noisy, too.
5. Roy joined the other noisy boys.
6. The boys wanted coins to buy more toys.
7. Roy said: "Let's annoy everyone with our noise.
8. The annoyed ones will give us coins to stop."
9. Neighbors threw moist oil, not coins.
10. The oily, soiled boys were much less noisy.

### TONGUE TWISTER

Toys are enjoyed by
girls and boys.
Oily, noisy toys
are not enjoyed.
The best toys are
not oily or soiled.

### LIMERICK

A man, Mr. Choy, liked to toil.
And work all day in the soil.
When home came Choy,
His wife showed much joy,
And stir-fried his food in hot
   oil.

## THE DIPHTHONG SOUND [aʊ]-/aʊ/-(ou)

 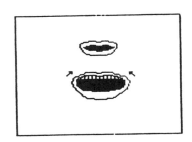

### DESCRIPTION

The phoneme [aʊ]-/aʊ/-(ou) is the low-back lax to high-back diphthong sound. It is produced in the following manner:

1. The back of the tongue is raised slightly in the back of the mouth toward the soft palate, as in sound [a].
2. The mouth is nearly wide open.
3. The lips are neutral.
4. Air is exhaled through the closed vocal folds, causing phonation.
5. As the sound is started, the jaw moves to the nearly closed position, the lips become rounded, and the back of the tongue moves close to the soft palate, toward the position for the phoneme [u]-/uʏ-(ōō).

### SPELLINGS

The [aʊ]-/aʊ/-(ou) sound is spelled in these ways:

> "ou" as in "south"
> "ow" as in "now"

### PROBLEMS

The most common problem with the phoneme [aʊ]-/aʊ/-(ou) is incompleteness. Often, the sound's movement phase is not finished, so that "doubt" sounds like "Dot," or "pout" like "pot."

[aʊ]                           /aʊ/                            ou

## PRACTICE A - WORDS

| | | | | | |
|---|---|---|---|---|---|
| OUnce | abOUt | cOUnt | lOUd | sOUnd | allOW |
| OUt | arOUnd | crOWd | mOUnt | sOUth | bOW |
| OUtdoors | brOWn | dOWn | mOUth | tOWn | cOW |
| OUtline | clOUd | fOUnd | pOUnd | vOWel | hOW |
| OWl | compOUnd | hOUse | shOUt | withOUt | nOW |

## PRACTICE B - CONTRASTS

| | | | |
|---|---|---|---|
| bOUnd-bond | dOUbt-dot | pOUnd-pond | spOUt-spot |
| bOUt-bot | dOWn-Don | plOWed-plod | tOUt-tot |
| brOWns-bronze | fOUnd-fond | pOUt-pot | wOUnd-wand |
| clOUd-clod | **fount-font** | scOUt-Scot | hOW-hah |
| dOWn-Don | gOUt-got | shOUt-shot | pOW-pa |

## PRACTICE C - SENTENCE CONTRASTS

1. I'm bOUnd by my bond.
2. Don fell dOWn.
3. **Don't pOUnd by a pond.**
4. He's got the gOUt.
5. The Scot is a scOUt.
6. The spOUt has a spot.
7. TrOUt swim, not trot.
8. It's wOUnd on a wand.
9. Say: "How," not "Hah."
10. My pa said: "Pow!"

## PRACTICE D - SENTENCES

1. About three hours ago, Mr. Brown went down town.
2. **He growled about the loud down town crowds.**
3. Brown liked the outstanding down town  bargains.
4. He went to the south side of the down town area.
5. Brown walked around for about two hours.
6. He found a dark brown night gown for Mrs. Brown.
7. Mrs. Brown shouted vowels loudly at seeing it.
8. "Get the brown gown out of the house," she said.
9. Brown went out and put the gown on a brown cow.
10. Now, Brown won't go down town for night gowns.

### TONGUE TWISTER

An owl shouted
loudly at the crowd.
"Loud shouting foul
mouthed owls should
get out of town,"
the crowd yowled.

### LIMERICK

A mountaineer named Blount
Always climbs the high mount.
With his head in the clouds,
He's out of the crowds.
Blount has to make every step
    count.

61

## SUMMARY

The three diphthong sounds, [aɪ]–/aɪ/–(ī), [ɔɪ]–/ɔɪ/–(oi) and [aʊ]–/aʊ/–(ou), require large movements of the articulators for accurate production. The tongue and jaw move from open to closed positions, as the lips become more spread or rounded. If you make these actions slowly and carefully, you will be able to produce these sounds correctly.

CHAPTER 6

# CONSONANT SOUNDS

Twenty-five (25) separate phonemes are included in the list of consonants. They may be catagorized in five groups: <u>plosives</u>, <u>fricatives</u>, <u>africates</u>, <u>glides</u> and <u>nasals</u>. Each of these terms describes the manner in which the phonemes are produced. This is illustrated in the Consonant Chart (Chart 6.1).

## PLOSIVES

Each of the six sounds listed as plosives is produced with the same <u>manner of articulation</u> (way of being made). Two articulators come together, block the air from <u>exiting</u> (leaving) the mouth. Air is exhaled and builds up pressure behind the block. The block is released suddenly, making a popping sound as the air "explodes" from the mouth.

## FRICATIVES

These nine sounds have a different manner of articulation than the plosives. They are produced by squeezing exhaled air out of the mouth through a narrow <u>channel</u> (opening). Two articulators are brought close together, but not totally touching, as they do for plosives. The breath stream passes between them, much like air that is pushed through an air pump. A hissing noise is heard, resulting from the friction between the sides of the channel and the moving air.

| PHONEME | PLACE OF ARTICULATION | VOICING | TYPE |
|---|---|---|---|
| [p]-(p)<br>[b]-(b) | LIP TO LIP | VOICELESS<br>VOICED | PLOSIVE |
| [t]-(t)<br>[d]-(d) | TONGUE TIP<br>TO GUM RIDGE | VOICELESS<br>VOICED | PLOSIVE |
| [k]-(k)<br>[g]-(g) | TONGUE BACK TO<br>SOFT PALATE | VOICELESS<br>VOICED | PLOSIVE |
| [f]-(f)<br>[v]-(v) | LOWER LIP TO<br>UPPER TEETH | VOICELESS<br>VOICED | FRICATIVE |
| [θ]-(th)<br>[ð]-(th) | TONGUE TIP<br>TO TEETH | VOICELESS<br>VOICED | FRICATIVE |
| [s]-(s)<br>[z]-(z) | TONGUE BLADE<br>TO GUM RIDGE | VOICELESS<br>VOICED | FRICATIVE |
| [ʃ]-(sh)<br>[ʒ]-(zh) | TONGUE FRONT TO<br>FRONT PALATE | VOICELESS<br>VOICED | FRICATIVE |
| [h]-(h) | GLOTTIS | VOICELESS | FRICATIVE |
| [ʧ]-(ch)<br>[ʤ]-(j) | TONGUE FRONT TO<br>FRONT PALATE | VOICELESS<br>VOICED | AFRICATE |
| [hw]-(hw)<br>[w]-(w) | LIP TO LIP | VOICELESS<br>VOICED | GLIDE |
| [j]-(y) | TONGUE FRONT TO<br>FRONT PALATE | VOICED | GLIDE |
| [l]-(l) | TONGUE TIP<br>TO GUM RIDGE | VOICED | GLIDE |
| [r]-(r) | TONGUE CENTER<br>TO PALATE | VOICED | GLIDE |
| [m]-(m) | LIP TO LIP | VOICED | NASAL |
| [n]-(n) | TONGUE TIP<br>TO GUM RIDGE | VOICED | NASAL |
| [ŋ]-(ng) | TONGUE BACK TO<br>SOFT PALATE | VOICED | NASAL |

Chart 6.1 - CONSONANTS

# AFRICATES

The two africate sounds, as their name suggests, have a fricative element in them. They actually combine the actions of a plosive and a fricative. First the breath stream is blocked and pressure built up. Then the block is released, but through a narrow channel that is created by squeezing the tongue against the palate.

# GLIDES

The word glide implies a smooth movement, as a skater gliding across the ice. Similarly, the five glide phonemes are produced as the articulators glide from one position to another. As with the diphthongs, these sounds start with the articulators in one position and move to another. If the glide sound is at the beginning of a word, the articulators start in its position and move away from it. If the phoneme is at the end or the middle of a word, the articulators start somewhere else and move toward its position.

# NASALS

The three nasal sounds, as the word suggests, have something to do with the nose. Specifically, the breath stream is blocked by the articulators from leaving the mouth. The soft palate is lowered, allowing the air to enter the nasal pasageways and flow outward through the openings in the nose.

# PLACE OF ARTICULATION

For each of the consonant sounds, a specific place of articulation is listed. This indicates the two articulators which either touch or come close together to produce the particular sound. In the case of the glide sounds, it indicates the starting or ending positions for these phonemes.

# VOICING

All of the vowel and diphthong sounds are produced with voicing (vocal fold vibration), but some of the consonants are not. They are called

65

voiceless consonants.   The others are voiced.

## COGNATES

Many consonants are   pairs, for example  [t] and
[d].     Each   has   the   same  place  and  manner   of
articulation,    but the [t]  is voiceless, while   the
[d] is voiced.   These two sounds, among others,   form
a cognate  pair, that is,   they are closely   related.
The  primary  difference  between  the members  of  a
cognate  pair, like  the  [t] and  [d],  is  voicing.
Other cognates,   for example, are:   [k] and [g],  [s]
and [z], and [hw] and [w].

## THE CONSONANT SOUND [p]-/p/-(p)

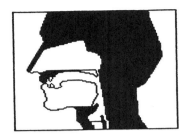
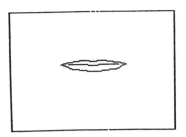

## DESCRIPTION

The phoneme [p] is the voiceless lip to lip plosive consonant. It is produced in the following manner:
1.  The lips are closed, preventing air from escaping from the mouth.
2.  Air is exhaled through the open vocal folds.
3.  Air pressure builds up within the mouth.
4.  The lips are moved quickly apart, allowing the air to explode from the mouth.
5.  A small puff of air can be felt at the moment of release. The air must be heard between the [p] and the following sound.
6.  If the following sound is another plosive, the air is blocked by the lips. Retaining the seal, the articulators are moved to the position of the next sound and then the air is exploded, for example: "popcorn" or "captain".

## SPELLINGS

The following spellings result in the [p] sound:

"gh" as in "hiccough"
"p" as in "prop"
"pp" as in "happy"

## PROBLEMS

The [p] may be omitted so that "soap" sounds like "so," or "soup" sounds like "sue." The [b] may be substituted so that "pack" sounds like "back," or "rope" sounds like "robe."

[p]                                    /p/                                    p

## PRACTICE A - WORDS

| Page  | Picture | aPPear    | paPer   | droP  | shiP |
|-------|---------|-----------|---------|-------|------|
| Paper | Poor    | coPy      | perhaPs | grouP | soaP |
| Part  | Pull    | haPPy     | rePort  | helP  | toP  |
| Past  | Push    | imPortant | simPle  | hoPe  | tyPe |
| Pay   | Put     | oPen      | uPon    | keeP  | uP   |

## PRACTICE B - CONTRASTS

| leaP-lea   | Panned-banned | moPPing-mobbing | cuP-cub |
|------------|---------------|-----------------|---------|
| seeP-see   | Paste-baste   | naPPing-nabbing | coP-cob |
| roPe-row   | Pin-been      | rumPle-rumble   | gaP-gab |
| hooP-who   | Polled-bold   | staPle-stable   | laP-lab |
| crouP-crew | Pun-bun       | simPle-symbol   | riP-rib |

## PRACTICE C - SENTENCE CONTRASTS

1. I'll keeP the key.
2. Who has the hooP?
3. It's a Pace to base.
4. I bail with a Pail.
5. Buy a new back Pack.
6. StaPle it to a stable.
7. Use the simPle symbol.
8. The cub broke a cuP.
9. Use a robe roPe on it.
10. We suP on the sub.

## PRACTICE D - SENTENCES

1. Many people like to play with puppies.
2. A happy little puppy is a pleasent pet.
3. Purchasing a puppy takes careful planning.
4. A trip to a pet shop is most important.
5. One should preview pictures before purchasing.
6. The puppy that can sleep on your lap may grow.
7. It is not cheap to keep a puppy.
8. Pet food and supplies keep pockets empty.
9. Plan to spend plenty to repair puppy damage.
10. Puppies bring pleasure, but also responsibility.

### TONGUE TWISTER

Peter Piper picked a peck of pickled peppers. Where is the peck of pickled peppers that Peter Piper picked?

### LIMERICK

My papa jumped up from a nap
To see a peppy pup in his lap.
Said papa, "don't nip me,
Or with your teeth grip me,
Or papa will give you a rap.

## THE CONSONANT SOUND [b]-/b/-(b)

 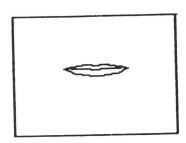

### DESCRIPTION

The phoneme [b] is a voiced, lip to lip plosive sound. It is produced in the following manner:
1. The lips are closed lightly together.
2. Air is exhaled through the lightly closed vocal folds, causing phonation.
3. Voiced air pressure builds up inside the mouth.
4. The lips are suddenly opened, so that the voiced air explodes from the mouth.
5. Little or no air escapes between the [b] phoneme and the following sound.
6. If the [b] is followed by another plosive, the lips block the air, the articulators move to the position of the following sound. The explosion takes place there.

### SPELLINGS

The following spellings result in the [b] sound:

"b" as in "bib"
"bb" as in "rubber"

### PROBLEMS

The [b] may be omitted from the end of a word so that "tribe" sounds like "try," or "robe" sounds like "row." Two frequent substitutions are [p] and [v], so that "cob" sounds like "cop," or "berry" sounds like "very."

[b]                          /b/                          b

## PRACTICE A - WORDS

| Back     | Before | aBout   | proBaBly | BiB      | laB   |
|----------|--------|---------|----------|----------|-------|
| Bad      | Big    | baBy    | possiBle | caB      | roBe  |
| Be       | Boy    | memBer  | rememBer | craB     | ruB   |
| Because  | But    | numBer  | suBject  | descriBe | tuB   |
| Been     | By     | proBlem | taBle    | joB      | tuBe  |

## PRACTICE B - CONTRASTS

| Back-pack     | staBle-staple | Berry-very         |
|---------------|---------------|--------------------|
| Bath-path     | roBe-roPe     | Boat-vote          |
| Beach-peach   | taB-tap       | cuPBoard-covered   |
| Big-pig       | Ban-van       | caB-calve          |
| symBol-simple | Bend-vend     | curB-curve         |

## PRACTICE C - SENTENCE CONTRASTS

1. Do Bears eat pears?
2. I have a Back pack.
3. It's a simple symBol.
4  We'll sup on the suB.
5. The vet made a Bet.

6. Your vest is Best.
7. I see a Bent vent.
8. We vote on the Boat.
9. Curves have curBs.
10. I rove in my roBe.

## PRACTICE D - SENTENCES

1. If you go back packing, be prepared for bears.
2. Bears are big and belligerent.
3. Never get between a bear cub and its mother.
4  Mother bear may believe you will grab the cub.
5. Bears will gobble up all eatables you bring.
6. Tying food bags above ground is best.
7. Keeping eatables near your bed area is bad.
8. A big bear may believe the food to be you.
9. Bears bring problems because they are beasts.
10. The best back pack trips are bearless ones.

### TONGUE TWISTER

Betty Beacham bought a
batch of bitter butter.
The butter made her
batter bitter. If Betty
buys better butter, her
batter won't be bitter.

### LIMERICK

Barry, a baker from Kerry,
Baked big pies of berry.
If his pies you buy,
You'll know, by and by
Berry pies taste better
     than cherry.

THE CONSONANT SOUND [t]-/t/-(t)

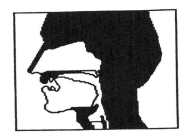
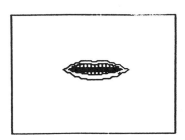

## DESCRIPTION

The phoneme [t] is the voiceless tongue tip to gum-ridge plosive consonant. It is produced in the following manner:
1. The tongue tip is placed against the gum-ridge blocking the air from exiting the mouth.
2. Air is exhaled through the open vocal folds and pressure builds up behind the tongue.
3. The tongue is quickly released from the gum-ridge allowing the air to explode from the mouth.
4. A small puff of air is allowed to escape before the following sound.
5. If the following sound is another plosive, the air is blocked by the tongue tip. Retaining the seal, the articulators are moved to the position for the next sound and the air is exploded.

## SPELLINGS

The following spellings result in the [t] sound:

"bt" as in "subtle"      "phth" as in "phthisic"
"cht" as in "yacht"      "pt" as in "receipt"
"d" as in "parked"       "th" as in Thailand"
"ght" as in "sight"      "t" as in "taste"
          "tt" as in "little"

## PROBLEMS

The [t] may be omitted so that "past" sounds like "pass," or "wait" sounds like "way." The [d] is often substituted so that "matter" resembles "madder". It may be made in a manner similar to the [θ]-/θ/-(th) that "tin" sounds something like "thin."

72

[t]                    /t/                              t

## PRACTICE A - WORDS

| | | (d) | | | |
|---|---|---|---|---|---|
| Table | To | beTTer | inTo | abouT | iT |
| Ten | Today | beTween | iTs | aT | noT |
| Test | laTer | cerTain | laTer | buT | ouT |
| Tight | Trees | ciTy | unTil | firsT | parT |
| Time | Two | counTry | waTer | geT | thaT |

(d)

## PRACTICE B - CONTRASTS

| | | | |
|---|---|---|---|
| liGHT-lie | liTer-leader | Tin-thin | tenT-tenth |
| raTe-ray | raTer-raider | Tree-three | boaT-both |
| Time-dime | wriTer-rider | deBTs-deaths | hearT-hearth |
| Ten-den | Tank-thank | eaTer-ether | paT-path |
| Ton-done | Team-theme | baTs-baths | sheeT-sheath |

## PRACTICE C - SENTENCE CONTRASTS

1. Ray knows the raTe.
2. I see the seaT
3. Give a dime in Time.
4. Its a meTal medal.
5. The bride is briGHT.
6. The kid made a kiT.
7. We need a neaT place.
8. The Tin is thin.
9. Say it with wiT.
10. It's the fourth forT.

## PRACTICE D - SENTENCES

1. Peter and Kate take their tent to the mountains.
2. Peter takes time to find the right tenting spot.
3. He tries to select the flattest site.
4. Pete trenches the site to prevent water damage.
5. After putting up the tent Pete takes a rest.
6. At the same time, Kate gets something to eat.
7. They sit, eat and watch the beautiful sunset.
8. Pete's and Kate's favorite time is twilight.
9. They take a trail to a tiny mountain meadow.
10. Kate takes photos of the timid rabbits there.

### TONGUE TWISTER

Tina, the toe tapper, tapped 'til ten. Tom, the tenant in the next apartment asked Tina not to tap late, so Tina taps 'till eight.

### LIMERICK

A talented tailor, Ted Zest,
Makes suits to fit the best.
He'll toil through the night
To get the fit right.
He makes the best vest in the
West.

73

## THE CONSONANT SOUND [d]-/d/-(d)

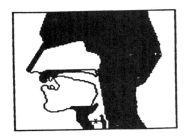
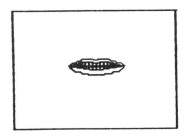

### DESCRIPTION

The phoneme [d] is the voiced tongue tip to gum-ridge plosive consonant. It is produced in the following manner:
1. The tongue tip is placed against the gum-ridge blocking the air from exiting the mouth.
2. Air is exhaled through the lightly closed vocal folds, causing phonation.
3. Voiced air builds up pressure within the mouth.
4. The tongue is released quickly from the gum-ridge allowing the air to explode from the mouth.
5. A small puff of air can be felt at the moment of release, but it is much weaker than for the [t]. No air can be heard between it and the following sound.
6. If the following sound is another plosive, the air is blocked by the tongue tip. Retaining the seal, the articulators are moved to the position for the next sound and then the air is exploded.

### SPELLINGS

The following spellings result in the [d] sound:

> "d" as in "dyed"
> "dd" as in "middle"

### PROBLEMS

The [d] may be omitted so that "grade" sounds like "gray," or "tide" sounds like "tie." The [t] may be substituted so that "ladder" resembles "latter." It may be made similar to the sound [ð]-/ð/-(th) so that "den" sounds like "then."

[d]                              /d/                              d

## PRACTICE A - WORDS

| | | | | | |
|---|---|---|---|---|---|
| Day | Do | chilDren | orDer | anD | maDe |
| Did | Don't | coulDn't | toDay | calleD | olD |
| Didn't | Does | hunDred | unDer | coulD | saiD |
| Died | Down | iDea | worDs | finD | sounD |
| Different | During | miDDle | wonDer | haD | woulD |

## PRACTICE B - CONTRASTS

| | | |
|---|---|---|
| finD-fine | traDer-traitor | Day-they |
| graDe-gray | baD-bat | Dough-though |
| raiD-ray | haD-hat | riDing-writhing |
| Dime-time | neeD-neat | laiD-lathe |
| beDDing-betting | saD-sat | sueD-soothe |

## PRACTICE C - SENTENCE CONTRASTS

1. I'll traDe a tray.
2. We see the seeD.
3. Put ten in the Den.
4. We've eaten in EDen.
5. That's a baD bat.
6. He'll senD you a cent.
7. Go to the Den, then.
8. They had a good Day.
9. Father bought foDDer.
10. I laiD it on a lathe.

## PRACTICE D - SENTENCES

1. Don and Dora loved diving.
2. Don had won many diving medals.
3. Dora hadn't won medals, but was a good diver.
4. Don did his diving from the high board.
5. Dora did her dives from the low board.
6. One day, Don was offered a daring job.
7. He would do some dangerous diving.
8. He would dive down one hundred feet into a pool.
9. Dora doubted that Don would do it.
10. Now Don does dangerous dives daily; Dora reads.

### TONGUE TWISTER

David, the dreamer,
dreamed daily down
at the drug store.
David's dreams delt
with the dangers of
diving and driving.

### LIMERICK

Here lived old Doctor Dill.
He cured disease with a pill.
He delivered a hug
With each dispensed drug.
Drugs and hugs are good when
    you're ill.

75

## THE CONSONANT SOUND [k]-/k/-(k)

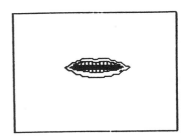

### DESCRIPTION

The phoneme [k] is the voiceless tongue back to soft palate plosive consonant. It is produced in the following manner:

1. The back of the tongue is raised to the soft palate, blocking the air from exiting the mouth.
2. Air is exhaled through the open vocal folds.
3. The air builds up pressure within the mouth.
4. The tongue is pulled quickly from the soft palate allowing the air to explode from the mouth.
5. A puff of air is felt and heard at the moment of release between it and the following sound.
6. If the following sound is another plosive, the air is blocked by the tongue back. Retaining the seal, the articulators are moved to the position for the next sound and then the air is exploded.

### SPELLINGS

The following spellings result in the [k] sound:

"c" as in "car"          "k" as in "kick"
 cc" as in "acclaim"     "q" as in "quit"
"ch" as in "ache"        "que" as in "bisque"
"ck" as in "back"        "x",[ks], as in "six"

### PROBLEMS

The [k] may be omitted so that "steak" sounds like "stay," or "bike" sounds like "buy." The [g] may be substituted so that "curl" resembles "girl." or "back" sounds like "bag."

76

[k]                           /k/                                    k

## PRACTICE A - WORDS

| | | | | | |
|---|---|---|---|---|---|
| Called | Complete | aCt | eQual | baCK | maKe |
| Can | Copy | aCross | looKing | blaCK | marK |
| Cause | Could | broKen | reCord | laKe | milK |
| Cold | Kept | disCover | sKin | liKe | speaK |
| Come | Key | doCtor | unCle | looK | worK |

## PRACTICE B - CONTRASTS

| | | | |
|---|---|---|---|
| baKe-bay | Call-gall | biCKer-bigger | baCK-bag |
| biKe-buy | Came-game | deCree-degree | buCK-bug |
| liKe-lie | Could-good | piCKy-piggy | duCK-dug |
| maKe-may | Card-guard | taCKing-tagging | piCK-pig |
| seeK-see | Come-gum | saCKing-sagging | raCK-rag |

## PRACTICE C - SENTENCE CONTRASTS

1. Lay it in the laKe.
2. Ask Ray for a raKe.
3. Stay for a steaK.
4. He Curls girls hair.
5. The gold is Cold.
6. A guard took a Card.
7. It's muggy and muCKy.
8. DiCK will dig it.
9. Doug has a duCK.
10. Put the bag in baCK.

## PRACTICE D - SENTENCES

1. Karen and Kiko are companions at college.
2. Karen is completing a chemistry course.
3. Kiko is concentrating on computer technology.
4. They are acquainted with many campus characters.
5. They frequently converse on complex subjects.
6. A common topic is politics.
7. Republican, democrat or communist, they talk.
8. Week in and week out, they collect and converse.
9. Talking keeps them thirsty, so they drink Cokes.
10. When the talks conclude, each is contented.

### TONGUE TWISTER

Becky the baker baked
cookies in a clean
kitchen. Said Becky
to Jack the kitchen
cleaner, "A carefully
cleaned kitchen is keen.

### LIMERICK

In L.A., the county shakes
From occasional quakes.
The quake checkers say,
"One could come any day."
Keeping calm there great
courage takes.

77

THE CONSONANT SOUND [g]-/g/-(g)

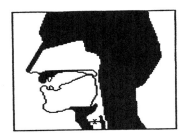
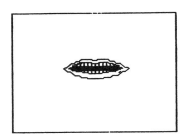

## DESCRIPTION

The phoneme [g] is the voiced tongue back to soft palate plosive consonant. It is produced in the following manner:
1. The tongue back is set against the soft palate, blocking the air from exiting the mouth.
2. Air is exhaled through the lightly closed vocal folds, causing phonation.
3. Voiced air builds up pressure within the mouth.
4. The tongue is moved quickly from the soft palate, allowing the air to explode from the mouth.
5. A small puff of air can be felt at the moment of release, but it is much weaker than for the [k]. No air can be heard between it and the following sound.
6. If the following sound is another plosive, the air is blocked by the tongue back. Keeping the seal, the articulators are moved to the position for the next sound and then the air is exploded.

## SPELLINGS

The following spellings result in the [g] sound:

"g" as in "give"          "gh" as in "ghost"
"gg" as in "bigger"       "x" as in "exactly"

## PROBLEMS

The [g] may be omitted so that "league" sounds like "lea," or "rogue" sounds like "row." The [k] may be substituted so that "good" resembles "could," or "bag" sounds like "back."

[g]                    /g/                        g

## PRACTICE A - WORDS

| Gas   | Good   | aGain   | finGer    | baG   | leG  |
|-------|--------|---------|-----------|-------|------|
| Get   | Got    | aGainst | sinGle    | biG   | loG  |
| Give  | Great  | anGle   | suGar     | doG   | piG  |
| Go    | Group  | beGin   | suGgest   | flaG  | ruG  |
| Gold  | Ground | eXactly | toGether  | foG   | taG  |

## PRACTICE B - CONTRASTS

| leaGUE-lea   | Gassed-cast  | Gold-cold     | deGree-decree   |
|--------------|--------------|---------------|-----------------|
| loG-law      | GHoul-cool   | Got-cot       | baG-back        |
| Game-came    | Glad-clad    | Great-crate   | biGGer-bicker   |
| Gain-cane    | Glean-clean  | Grow-crow     | buG-buck        |
| Guard-card   | Glue-clue    | Gum-come      | flaG-flack      |

## PRACTICE C - SENTENCE CONTRASTS

1.  Lee walked a leaGue.        6.  The baG is out back.
2.  There's a roGue row.        7.  Its a buck for a buG.
3.  Come get the Gum.           8.  A duck bit DouG.
4   Kate closed the Gate.       9.  We need a raG rack.
5.  That's a picky piGGy.      10.  Put a tack on a taG.

## PRACTICE D - SENTENCES

1.  Gus and his girl, Gail, love the game of golf.
2.  Gus is a good golfer, but Gail is greater.
3.  In August, Gus shot a double bogey.
4.  Gail got a double eagle.
5.  One day, Gus went to get Gail to go golfing.
6.  Gail wanted to get golfing togs, first.
7.  Gus got angry while Gail got the goods.
8.  When they got to play golf, Gus was no good.
9.  Gail got an eagle, while Gus got another bogey .
10.  Now we know why Gail plays better golf than Gus.

### TONGUE TWISTER

Gary is a good
gardener. He grows
big gardenias. Bugs
gobble gardenias, so
Gary gets ugly bugs
out of the garden.

### LIMERICK

I gave some gold to Glen
To bet on the race to win.
The nag didn't go.
It galloped so slow,
And now, I'm broke again.

79

## THE CONSONANT SOUND [f]-/f/-(f)

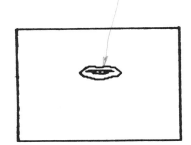

### DESCRIPTION

The phoneme [f] is the voiceless lower lip to upper teeth fricative consonant. It is produced in the following manner:
1. The lower lip moves back and under the upper teeth.
2. The jaw closes, bringing the upper front teeth in contact with the lower lip.
3. Air is exhaled through the open vocal folds.
4. The voiceless breath stream passes through the mouth and is forced out between the upper teeth and lower lip.

### SPELLINGS

The following spellings result in the [f] sound:

"f" as in "fast"
"ff" as in "cuff"
"ft" as in "often"
"gh" as in "cough"
"ph" as in "phone"

### PROBLEMS

The [f] may be omitted from the ends of words, so that "beef" sounds like "be," or "knife" like "nigh." The sound [p] may be substituted, so that "fine" sounds like "pine," or "fast" like "past." The [v] sound may also intrude, so that "fat" sounds like "vat."

[f]                         /f/                              f

## PRACTICE A - WORDS

| Father | Food  | aFter       | leFt  | chieF    | oFF      ← |
|--------|-------|-------------|-------|----------|------------|
| Far    | For   | beautiFul   | liFe  | enouGH   | paragraPH  |
| Few    | Form  | beFore      | liFt  | himselF  | saFe       |
| Find   | Found | diFFerent   | oFTen | iF       | yourselF   |
| Follow | From  | inFormation | soFt  | lauGH    | wiFe       |

## PRACTICE B - CONTRASTS

| oFF-awe      | Face-pace  | Four-pour       | Face-vase  |
|--------------|------------|-----------------|------------|
| beeF-bee     | Far-par    | Fun-pun         | Fast-vast  |
| kniFe-nigh   | Fast-past  | lauGHed-lapped  | Fat-vat    |
| leaF-Lee     | Fat-pat    | lauGHs-laps     | Few-view   |
| saFe-say     | Feel-peel  | wiFe-wipe       | Fine-vine  |

## PRACTICE C - SENTENCE CONTRASTS

1.  Can that be beeF?
2.  Lee lost the leaF.
3.  "I'm saFe," I say!
4   She ran past, Fast.
5.  Pour Four shakes.
6.  Telling a pun is Fun.
7.  My wiFe will wipe it.
8.  Now, Face the vase.
9.  A Few have a view.
10. What a Fine vine.

## PRACTICE D - SENTENCES

1.  Frank and Fae file fashion reports for a paper.
2.  Fae writes of fancy, fabulous, female fashions.
3.  Frank follows fashion trends for fellows.
4.  Frank often finds fashion fads to be funny.
5.  Fae feels female fashions should be functional.
6.  Fae and Frank flew to France for a fashion show.
7.  They found fine food and fantastic fun.
8.  They forgot fashions and had a few laughs.
9.  They finally filled paragraphs with fashions.
10. Satisfied, they flew off to Philadelphia.

### TONGUE TWISTER

Fran Farmer found
forty fitful flies
flitting after four
beautiful fillies.
She flicked the flies
off of the fillies.

### LIMERICK

If a fellow helps his wife,
And dries each fork and knife,
If they join forces,
The result, of course is,
Fine feelings for an eternal
   life.

81

THE CONSONANT SOUND [v]-/v/-(v)

     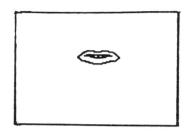

DESCRIPTION

The phoneme [v] is the voiced lower lip to upper teeth fricative consonant. It is produced in the following manner:
1.  The lower lip moves back and under the upper teeth.
2.  The jaw closes, bringing the upper front teeth in contact with the lower lip.
3.  Air is exhaled through the closed vocal folds, producing phonation.
4.  The voiced breath stream passes through the mouth and is forced out between the upper teeth and lower lip.

SPELLINGS

The following spellings result in the [v] sound:

"f" as in "of"
"v" as in "vacation"

PROBLEMS

The [v] may be omitted from the ends of words, so that "save" sounds like "say," or "dive" like "dye." The sound [b] may be substituted, so that "vote" sounds like "boat," or "vie" like "by". The sound [f] may intrude, so that "vat" sounds like "fat." The phoneme [w] may be used so that "very" sounds like "wary".

[v]                            /v/                              v

## PRACTICE A - WORDS

| | | | | | |
|---|---|---|---|---|---|
| Valley | View | coVer | neVer | belieVe | liVe |
| Value | Village | eVen | riVer | driVe | loVe |
| Variety | Visit | eVer | seVeral | fiVe | moVe |
| Verb | Voice | eVery | traVel | giVe | oF |
| Very | Vowel | howeVer | waVes | haVe | solVe |

## PRACTICE B - CONTRASTS

| | | | |
|---|---|---|---|
| diVe-die | Van-ban | curVe-curb | Van-fan |
| leaVe-Lee | Very-berry | roVe-robe | Very-ferry |
| liVe-lie | Vet-bet | Very-wary | saVer-safer |
| saVe-say | Vote-boat | Vet-wet | fiVe-fife |
| stoVe-stow | Vowel-bowel | Vine-wine | haVe-half |

## PRACTICE C - SENTENCE CONTRASTS

1.  Lee will leaVe.
2.  Don't lie!  It's liVe.
3.  "SaVe it," I say!
4   See the bat in a Vat.
5.  Bile is Vile.
6.  I'm Very wary.
7.  The Vet got wet.
8.  Put a fan in the Van.
9.  That's a fine Vine.
10. May I haVe half?

## PRACTICE D - SENTENCES

1.  Vivian Vance vowed to have a great vacation.
2.  She and Van would visit every valley in Vermont.
3.  They would view every village and vale.
4.  Never would they have a more varied vacation.
5.  They drove to Vermont in their Volvo.
6.  They traveled by several rivers.
7.  The Vances had a variety of adventures.
8.  Every curve had several valuable views.
9.  Even the best vacation, however, is short lived.
10. The Vances drove home after a lovely visit.

### TONGUE TWISTER

"Visit Virginia"
voiced the traveler.
"Virginia has my
vote.  It vibrates
with violets; it's
covered with rivers."

### LIMERICK

A very fine voter of note,
Once tried to alter his vote.
He has voted very badly
And was feeling very sadly.
He had voted for a vicious
   old goat.

## THE CONSONANT SOUND [θ]—/θ/—⟨th⟩

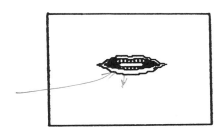

## DESCRIPTION

The phoneme [θ]—/θ/—⟨th⟩ is the voiceless tongue-tip to to teeth fricative consonant. It is produced in the following manner:
1. The tongue tip is placed between the front teeth.
2. The jaw is nearly closed.
3. Air is exhaled through the open vocal folds.
4. The voiceless breath stream passes through the mouth and is forced out between the upper teeth and the tongue tip.
5. As the breath is squeezed out through the narrow space between the tongue and teeth, the tongue is slowly pulled back into the mouth.
6. The breath stream flows continuously as the next sound is produced.
7. If the phoneme ends a word, the breath stream stops before the tongue is moved.

## SPELLINGS

The [θ]—/θ/—⟨th⟩ sound is spelled in this way:

"th" as in "thin"

## PROBLEMS

The most common problem with the [θ]—/θ/—(th) sound is substitution. Most frequently, the [t] is used so that "thank" sounds like "tank," or "booth" sounds like "boot." Using [s] is a common error, so that "think" sounds like "sink," or "bath" sounds like "bass." The sound [f] may also intrude so that "think" sounds like "fink."

[θ]                      / θ /                            th

## PRACTICE A - WORDS

| THank   | THird    | anyTHing    | maTHematics | beneaTH |
|---------|----------|-------------|-------------|---------|
| THick   | THirty   | auTHor      | meTHod      | boTH    |
| THin    | THought  | auTHority   | noTHing     | deaTH   |
| THings  | THousand | earTHquake  | someTHing   | earTH   |
| THink   | THree    | everyTHing  | souTHwest   | monTH   |

## PRACTICE B - CONTRASTS

| THank-tank   | baths-bats  | THank-sank | fourTH-force |
|--------------|-------------|------------|--------------|
| THeme-team   | fourTH-fort | THin-sin   | THin-fin     |
| THin-tin     | tenTH-tent  | THink-sink | THink-fink   |
| THrust-trust | tooTH-toot  | baTH-bass  | deaTH-deaf   |
| deaTHs-debts | wiTH-wit    | mouTH-mouse| myTH-miff    |

## PRACTICE C - SENTENCE CONTRASTS

1. THanks for the tanks.
2. That's THin tin.
3. Go to the boot booTH.
4  See the tenTH tent.
5. Speak wiTH wit.
6. Sing the THing.
7. Old THor got sore.
8. Don't pass the paTH.
9. THree are free.
10. Think of THirst first.

## PRACTICE D - SENTENCES

1. This earth is troubled with earthquakes.
2. Earthquakes occur beneath the earth's surface.
3. Men have thought about earth thousands of times.
4. Nothing (ever thought of) can stop an earthquake.
5. The thin earth's crust has many lengthy cracks.
6. Earth's forces thrust them up, causing shaking.
7. Earth shakes to the North, South, East and West.
8. Thoughtful thinkers think of survival methods.
9. A three day supply of needed things is minimum.
10. Think of the things you require for good health.

### TONGUE TWISTER

Thistle picker, Theo,
thrust thousands of
thistles into the
thick of his thumb
without thinking of
a thumb thimble.

### LIMERICK

As Theodore walked on a path,
Thoughtfully thinking of math,
He thrust a foot in a hole,
And in thick mud did roll.
Now Theodore's taking a bath.

## THE CONSONANT SOUND [ð]–/ð/–(th)

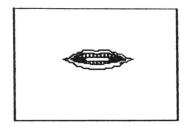

## DESCRIPTION

The phoneme [ð]–/ð/–(th) is the voiced tongue-tip to teeth fricative consonant. It is produced in the following manner:
1. The tongue tip is placed between the front teeth.
2. The jaw is nearly closed.
3. Air is exhaled through the closed vocal folds, causing phonation.
4. The voiced breath stream passes through the mouth and is forced out between the upper teeth and the tongue tip.
5. As the vibrated breath is squeezed out through the narrow space between the tongue and teeth, the tongue is slowly pulled back into the mouth.
6. The breath stream flows continuously as the next sound is produced.
7. If the sound ends a word, the breath stream stops before the tongue is moved.

## SPELLINGS

The [ð]–/ð/–(th) sound is spelled in this way:

"th" as in "this"

## PROBLEMS

The most common problem with the [ð]–/ð/–(th) sound is substitution. Most frequently, the [d] is used so that "their" sounds like "dare," or "tithe" sounds like "tide." Using [z] is a common error, also, so that "then" sounds like "Zen," or "teethe" like "tease". [θ]–/θ/–(th) may also intrude, so that "teethe" "sounds like "teeth." [v] is sometimes used so that "that" sounds like "vat."

[ð]                    /ð/                    th

## PRACTICE A - WORDS

| | | | | | |
|---|---|---|---|---|---|
| THan | THen | THey'd | alTHough | moTHer | wiTHout |
| THat | THere | THey'll | anoTHer | neiTHer | breaTHe |
| The | THerefore | THey're | broTHer | oTHer | cloTHe |
| THeir | THese | THose | eiTHer | weaTHer | smooTH |
| THem | THey | THough | faTHer | wheTHer | wiTH |

*same pronunciation.*

## PRACTICE B - CONTRASTS

| | | |
|---|---|---|
| THan-Dan | faTHer-fodder | THen-Zen |
| THeir-dare | oTHer-udder | cloTHing-closing |
| THen-den | breaTHe-breed | breaTHe-breeze |
| THey-day | THis'll-thistle | THan-van |
| THose-doze | eiTHer-ether | THat-vat |

## PRACTICE C - SENTENCE CONTRASTS

1. Put it in a den, THen.
2. THey had a good day.
3. THose like to doze.
4. FaTHer made fodder.
5. I laid it on a laTHe.
6. This'll be a thistle.
7. Is THy thigh hurt?
8. I'm loath to loaTHe.
9. Study Zen, THen.
10. Put it in THat vat.

## PRACTICE D - SENTENCES

1. Mothers and fathers don't have smooth lives.
2. They must work together all the time.
3. They must be there when their kids need them.
4. They must feed, bathe and clothe the children.
5. Breathing and teething problems keep them busy.
6. Clothing is rather costly, but they buy it.
7. The needs of the family, therefore, come first.
8. Mother and father need to rest from their work.
9. Either a northern or southern trip will do.
10. Whether here or there, parents are the best.

### TONGUE TWISTER

"Don't bother my
brother," said
Father to Mother."
Brother would rather
work with that
leather.

### LIMERICK

We must be kind to each other,
Treat each one like a brother.
If this thing we do,
Then this statement is true:
"We'll be happier than
another."

## THE CONSONANT SOUND [s]-/s/-(s)

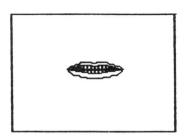

### DESCRIPTION

The phoneme [s] is the voiceless tongue tip to gum-ridge fricative consonant. It is produced in the following manner:
1. The center of the tongue tip is raised close to the gum ridge.
2. The sides of the tongue prevent air from exiting the mouth except to the front.
3. The jaw is nearly closed.
4. The lips are neutral.
5. Air is exhaled through the open vocal folds.
6. The voiceless breath stream passes through the mouth and is forced out between the tongue tip and the gum ridge, like the [z].

### SPELLINGS

The following spellings result in the [s] sound:

"c" as in "cent"          "ss" as in "less"
"ps" as in "psuedo"       "st as in "listen"
"s" as in "say"           "x," [ks], as in "box"
"sc" as in "science"      "z" as in "quartz"

### PROBLEMS

The most common problem with the phoneme [s] is substitution. The [θ]-/θ/-th) is used, so that "some" sounds like "thumb," or "face" like "faith." The [ʃ]-/ʃ/-(sh) may intrude, so that "said" sounds like "shed," or "plus" like "plush."

[s]                    /s/                          s

## PRACTICE A - WORDS

| | | | | | |
|---|---|---|---|---|---|
| Said | Set | beSide | neCeSSary | acroSS | pieCe |
| Same | So | conSonant | poSSible | faCe | plaCe |
| Say | Some | deCimal | reCeive | houSe | thiS |
| See | Sound | himSelf | themSelves | its | uS |
| Sentence | Such | liSTen | yourSelf | miSS | voiCe |

## PRACTICE B - CONTRASTS

| | | | |
|---|---|---|---|
| Saw-thaw | faCe-faith | Said-shed | faSTen-fashion |
| Seem-theme | forCe-fourth | Save-shave | laST-lashed |
| Sick-thick | kiSS-kith | See-she | claSS-clash |
| Sin-thin | mouSe-mouth | Self-shelf | meSS-mesh |
| Some-thumb | worSe-worth | So-show | pluS-plush |

## PRACTICE C - SENTENCE CONTRASTS

1. I Saw it thaw.
2. That thing can Sing.
3. I think it'll Sink.
4. It's no Sin I'm thin.
5. Go forth with forCe.

6. A tenth are tenSe.
7. A Sack is in a shack.
8. She can not See.
9. Bash that baSS!
10. The mesh is a meSS.

## PRACTICE D - SENTENCES

1. A successful business is one giving service.
2. Sam and Sue  own an auto service business.
3. Sam services cars and Sue keeps the office.
4. Seeing satisfied customers makes them serene.
5. Sam studies lots of books about servicing cars.
6. He makes certain he has sufficient supplies.
7. Sue's office has the latest business systems.
8. Customers are certain that costs are lowest.
9. They send their acquaintaces to Sam for service.
10. Sam and Sue will soon expand their business.

### TONGUE TWISTER

Sam and Sally sat
on the sofa, sipping
sodas silently.
Sally said: "Its
time to stop sipping
and start kissing."

### LIMERICK

Saul, a swimmer from Graster,
Daily, swam faster and faster.
His speed so fast rose,
He swam out of his clothes.
Now he sticks his suit on with
    plaster.

## THE CONSONANT SOUND [z]-/z/-(z)

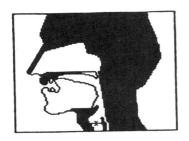 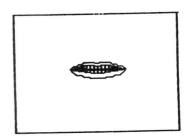

DESCRIPTION

The phoneme [z] is the voiced tongue tip to gum-ridge
fricative consonant.  It is produced in the following
manner:
1.  The center of the  tongue tip  is raised close to
    the gum-ridge.
2.  The sides of the tongue prevent air from  exiting
    the mouth except to the front.
3.  The jaw is nearly closed.
4.  The lips are neutral.
5.  Air is exhaled  through  the closed  vocal folds,
    causing phonation.
6.  The  voiced  breath  stream  passes  through  the
    mouth and is forced out between  the  tongue  tip
    and the gum ridge, like the [s].

SPELLINGS

    The following spellings result in the [z] sound:

"s" as in "tease"          "x" [gz] as in "exit"
"x" as in "Xerox"          "z" as in "lazy"
          "zz" as in "fuzzy"

PROBLEMS

    The most common problem  with  the phoneme [z] is
substitution.  The [s] is used, so that "zone" sounds
like "sewn", or "eyes" like "ice".  The  [ð]-/ð/-(th)
may be used, so  that  "Zen" sounds  like "then," or
"lays" like "lathe."  The sounds [d] may intrude,  at
the  end  of  a  word,  so  that  "rise"  sounds  like
"rides," or "buzz" sounds like "buds."

90

[z]                          /z/                              z

## PRACTICE A - WORDS

| | | | | | |
|---|---|---|---|---|---|
| Zero | deSign | preSent | aS | haS | theSe |
| Zone | eaSy | reaSon | cauSe | hiS | thoSE |
| Zoo | eXact | reSult | cloSe | iS | uSe |
| buSiness | eXample | waSn't | doeS | letterS | waS |
| deSert | obServe | alwayS | exerciSe | siZe | yearS |

## PRACTICE B - CONTRASTS

| | | | |
|---|---|---|---|
| Zip-sip | eyeS-ice | cloSe-clothe | buyS-bides |
| Zone-sewn | lieS-lice | layS-lathe | breeZe-breeds |
| Zoo-sue | loSe-loose | seas-seethe | goeS-goads |
| raZor-racer | Z-thee | siZe-scythe | siZe-sides |
| raiSes-races | Zen-then | tieS-tithes | tieS-tides |

## PRACTICE C - SENTENCE CONTRASTS

1. Zeke will seek you.
2. It's sewn in a Zone.
3. Sue went to the Zoo.
4. A racer has a raZor.
5. Put ice on his eyes.
6. It payS to pace fast.
7. Put sauce on the sawS!
8. It layS  on a lathe.
9. See a big siZe scythe.
10. You can't tithe tieS.

## PRACTICE D - SENTENCES

1. Visiting zoos is a pleasant way to use time.
2. Zack and Zoe are zoo workers.
3. Zack feeds animals and cares for their areas.
4. Zoe raises the zoo's babies and is always busy.
5. The zoo has many examples of endangered species.
6. Zack gives each the exact foods it requires.
7. Zoe observes the behaviors of the babies often.
8. She watches for causes of the animals diseases.
9. Good zoo workers make zoo visits always fun.
10. Zebras, lions, and bears are easily observed.

### TONGUE TWISTER

Zeke is a zipper
tester in zipper
factories.  Zeke
has zipped zippers
for years.  Zeke's
zippers always zip.

### LIMERICK

Being lazy is easy to do.
It needs no effort from you.
Do no exercises,
And you'll increase all sizes.
You'll raise pounds to six
    hundred and two.

91

## THE CONSONANT SOUND [ʃ]-/ʃ/-(sh)

  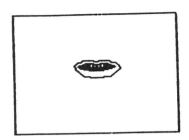

## DESCRIPTION

The phoneme [ʃ]-/ʃ/-(sh) is the voiceless tongue-blade to front palate fricative consonant. It is produced in the following manner:
1. The center of the tongue-blade is raised close to the front palate.
2. The sides of the tongue prevent air from exiting the mouth except to the front.
3. The jaw is nearly closed.
4. The lips are slightly rounded and pushed forward.
5. Air is exhaled through the open vocal folds.
6. The voiceless breath stream passes through the mouth and is forced out between the tongue blade and the front palate.

## SPELLINGS

The [ʃ]-/ʃ/-(sh) sound is spelled in these ways:

"ci" as in "special"       "ss" as in "issue"
"ch" as in "Chicago"       "ssi" as in "mission"
"s" as in "sugar"          "ti" as in "attention"
"sh" as in "shop"          "xi" as in "anxious"

## PROBLEMS

The [ʃ]-/ʃ/-(sh) is subject to errors of substitution, and addition. The [s] is substituted so that "ship" sounds like "sip," or "mash" like "mass." The [ʧ]/ʧ/-(ch) may be heard so that "sheep" sounds like "cheep," or "wash" like "watch." The sound [l]-/iʳ/-(ē) may be added to the final [ʃ]-/ʃ/-(sh), so that "fish" sounds like "fishy."

[ʃ]                          /ʃ/                              sh

## PRACTICE A - WORDS

| | | | | | |
|---|---|---|---|---|---|
| SHall | SHow | addiTIon | mission | aSH | diSH |
| SHarp | SHould | dicTIonary | naTIon | buSH | EngliSH |
| SHe | SHoulder | direcTIon | posiTIon | caSH | puSH |
| SHip | SHout | finiSHed | puSHed | cruSH | waSH |
| SHort | Sure | fracTIon | secTIon | daSH | wiSH |

## PRACTICE B - CONTRASTS

| | | |
|---|---|---|
| SHe-see | craSH-crass | maSHed-matched |
| SHeet-seat | puSH-puss | waSHed-watched |
| SHelf-self | SHeet-cheet | diSH-ditch |
| faSHion-fasten | SHe's-cheese | wiSH-witch |
| maSHes-masses | SHows-chose | fiSH-fishy |

## SENTENCE CONTRASTS

1. SHe can see it.
2. A SHeet is on a seat.
3. Sue has the SHoe.
4. Don't lease a leaSH.
5. MaSH a mass of peas.
6. I'll SHare the chair.
7. SHe's eating cheese.
8. Don't waSH the watch.
9. Witches have wiSHes.
10. Butch bought a buSH.

## PRACTICE D - SENTENCES

1. Shelley owns a fashionable shoe shop.
2. Shirley likes shopping for shoes at Shelley's.
3. She says Shelley's shoes surely are shapely.
4. His shelves aren't short of well finished shoes.
5. He ships shoes to all sections of the nation.
6. His shoe prices are a fraction of other shops.
7. My information is that Shelley once was shy.
8. Selling shoes pushed him in new directions.
9. His shoes are shown in international shops.
10. Shelley surely makes much cash with his shoes.

### TONGUE TWISTER

Shoppers push and
shove for shirts
and shoes in shops
with sales. They
crush and mash each
other as they rush.

### LIMERICK

In Chicago, a collector of trash
Wished to do something rash.
He showered and shaved,
And took cash he had saved,
And bought his wife a fur coat
    and sash.

93

## THE CONSONANT SOUND [ʒ]-/ʒ/-(zh)

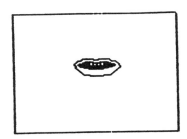

## DESCRIPTION

The phoneme [ʒ]-/ʒ/-(zh) is the voiced tongue-blade to front palate fricative consonant. It is produced in the following manner:
1. The center of the tongue-blade is raised close to the front palate.
2. The sides of the tongue prevent air from exiting the mouth except to the front.
3. The jaw is nearly closed.
4. The lips are slightly rounded and pushed forward.
5. Air is exhaled through the closed vocal folds, causing phonation.
6. The voiced breath stream passes through the mouth and is forced out between the tongue blade and the front palate.

## SPELLINGS

The [ʒ]-/ʒ/-(zh) sound is spelled in these ways:

"g" as in "garage"          "s" as in "treasure"
"j" as in "Bijou"           "si" as in "decision"
              "z" as in "azure"

## PROBLEMS

The most common problem with the [ʒ]-/ʒ/-(zh) substitution. The [ʃ]-/ʃ/-(sh) is used, so that "confusion" sounds like "Confucian." The [z] may intrude, so that "beige" sounds like "bays." The [dʒ]-/dʒ/(j) may be used, so that "measure" is said in a manner similar to, but not exactly like, "major."

[ʒ]                          /ʒ/                          zh

## PRACTICE A - WORDS

| | | | |
|---|---|---|---|
| confuSIon | garaGes | occaSIon | treaSure |
| deciSIon | meaSure | occaSIonally | unuSual |
| deciSIons | meaSured | pleaSure | unuSually |
| diviSIon | meaSures | pleaSures | uSual |
| diviSIons | meaSurement | televiSIon | garaGE |

## PRACTICE B - CONTRASTS

confuSion-Confucian     leiSure-leasher        beiGE-bays
glaZier-glacier         compoSure-composer     rouGE-ruse

## PRACTICE C - SENTENCE CONTRASTS

1. The Confucian shows confuSIon.
2. There's no glaZier on the glacier.
3. The leasher needed some leiSure.
4. The composer needs more compoSure.
5. Using rouGE is a ruse.

## PRACTICE D - SENTENCES

1. Leisure time is usually spent pleasurably.
2. Much leisure time is used watching television.
3. An unusual leisure activity is treasure hunting.
4. Hunting treasure is pleasurable and profitable.
5. A treasure hunting decision is not easy.
6. Occasionally, treasure is found under water.
7. Usually, measurable treasure is found on land.
8. The most usual decision is to search for gold.
9. Searching for gem stones is pleasurable leisure.
10. Don't make a casual decision about your leisure.

### TONGUE TWISTER

A Persian illusionist
creates confusion
with illusions. You
must measure all your
treasure after an
illusion confusion.

### LIMERICK

Zsa Zsa's unusual treasure
Usually gives much pleasure.
On television she's seen
As a beautiful queen.
Now that's a pleasure to
    measure.

95

## THE CONSONANT SOUND [h]-/h/-(h)

 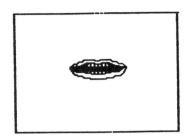

### DESCRIPTION

The phoneme [h] is the voiceless glottal fricative. It is produced in the following manner:
1. The mouth is opened to the position for the vowel sound in the word being uttered.
2. Air is exhaled through the open vocal folds.
3. The voiceless air stream passes through the mouth as in a whisper.

### SPELLINGS

The following spellings result in the [h] sound:

"h" as in "home"
"wh" as in "whole"

### PROBLEMS

The primary problem with the phoneme [h] is that of omission. Speakers from languages which have no [h], usually leave the sound off of words, so that "his" sounds like "is," or "head sounds like "Ed."

[h]                    /h/                          h

## PRACTICE A - WORDS

| Hair   | Have  | Held  | Hill    | Home  | aHead    |
|--------|-------|-------|---------|-------|----------|
| Hand   | He    | Help  | Him     | Hope  | beHave   |
| Happy  | Head  | Her   | His     | House | beHind   |
| Hard   | Hear  | Here  | History | WHo   | overHead |
| Has    | Heart | High  | Hole    | WHose | perHaps  |

## PRACTICE B - CONTRASTS

| Hair-heir | Hear-ear   | High-I    |
|-----------|------------|-----------|
| Hand-and  | Heart-art  | Hill-ill  |
| Has-as    | Heat-eat   | His-is    |
| Hat-at    | Heel-eel   | Hit-it    |
| Head-Ed   | Here-ear   | Hold-old  |

## PRACTICE C - SENTENCE CONTRASTS

1. My Hat is at school.
2. Ed has a good Head.
3. Hear with your ear.
4. Have a Heart, Art.
5. Heat it and eat it.
6. The eel bit my Heel.
7. I climbed High.
8. His cat is nice.
9. Don't Hit it.
10. It's too old to Hold.

## PRACTICE D - SENTENCES

1. Howard and Hannah Hope have a horse ranch.
2. Howard has the hard job of training the horses.
3. Hannah helps Howard with the hard work.
4. I have seen hundreds of their horses in movies.
5. Howard's training makes horses easy to handle.
6. Film heros and heroines hope to ride his horses.
7. Rehearsing horses takes heaps of Howard's time.
8. To get ahead with horses, the Hope's work hard.
9. The Hope's happiest times happen with horses.
10. Harold and Hannah are happy horse handlers.

### TONGUE TWISTER

Hank hammers nails
with a heavy hammer.
Hank's heavy hammer
is hard to handle.
Hank hits hundreds
of nail heads hard.

### LIMERICK

A hamster hawker, named Harry,
Has always hoped to marry.
But his sweetheart, Miss Hill,
Met a horse handler, Bill.
Now a broken heart Harry will
    carry.

97

## THE CONSONANT SOUND [ tʃ ]-/tʃ/-(ch)

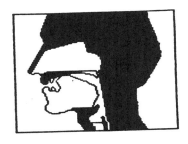
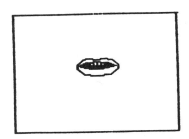

## DESCRIPTION

This is the phoneme [ tʃ ]-/tʃ/-(ch). It is a voiceless tongue-front to front-palate africate sound. It is produced in the following manner:
1. The front of the tongue is placed against the front-palate, blocking the breath stream.
2. The mouth is nearly closed.
3. The lips are slightly rounded and pushed forward.
4. Air is exhaled through the open vocal folds.
5. The voiceless breath stream builds up pressure.
6. **The tip of the tongue is lowered slightly and the breath stream explodes outward.**
7. The front of the tongue forces the breath stream through a narrow channel.

## SPELLINGS

The [ tʃ ]-/tʃ/-(ch) sound is spelled in the following ways:

"ch" as in "chair"          "tch" as in "catch"
"t" as in "future"          "te" as in "righteous"

## PROBLEMS

The [ tʃ ]-/tʃ/-(ch) sound may be substituted by the sound [ ʃ ]-/ʃ/-(sh), so that "choose" sounds like "shoes," or "ditch" like "dish." The [t] is heard so that "cheese" resembles "tease." At the ends of words, a vowel sound may be added, so that "itch" is produced like "itchy." The [ tʃ ]-/tʃ/-(ch) may be dropped from the end of a word, so that "beach" sounds like "bee." or "teach" like "tee."

98

[ tʃ ]                    / tʃ /                    ch

## PRACTICE A - WORDS

| | | | | | |
|---|---|---|---|---|---|
| CHair | CHief | cenTury | picTure | branCH | riCH |
| CHance | CHild | marCHed | reaCHed | caTCH | streTCH |
| CHange | CHina | maTCHing | searCHing | eaCH | suCH |
| CHarge | CHoose | naTural | strucTure | FrenCH | touCH |
| CHart | CHurch | naTure | teaCHer | muCH | whiCH |

## PRACTICE B - CONTRASTS

| | | |
|---|---|---|
| CHair-share | maTCHed-mashed | maTCHing-matting |
| CHeap-sheep | waTCHed-washed | caTCH-cat |
| CHeat-sheet | caTCH-cash | crunCH-crunchy |
| CHoose-shoes | diTCH-dish | iTCH-itchy |
| caTCHing-cashing | CHalk-talk | teaCH-tea |

## PRACTICE C - SENTENCE CONTRASTS

1.  May I share a CHair?
2.  Buy the CHeap sheep!
3.  He has a CHeat sheet.
4.  Try to caTCH cash.
5.  I waTCHed it washed.
6.  MarCH past the marsh.
7.  Give a CHalk talk.
8.  Take the coaCH a coat.
9.  She's a witchy wiTCH.
10. I'll be at the beaCH.

## PRACTICE D - SENTENCES

1.  Teaching children is a choice occupation.
2.  Charley and Rachel teach in Massachusetts.
3.  Teaching children is challenging.
4.  Each teacher has much work to do each day.
5.  Rachel teaches natural science and literature.
6.  Charles is a coach and teaches baseball.
7.  He helps pitchers pitch and catchers catch.
8.  The teachers didn't choose teaching for riches.
9.  They chose to teach searching minds to stretch.
10. They give structure to the future of each child.

### TONGUE TWISTER

Chuck, the chess
champ, chewed on
chicken, chocolate
chips and cherries
before checking in
at the chess match.

### LIMERICK

A child from the town of Birch
Went fishing to catch a perch.
When the child checked his line
His cheese bait was fine.
The perch had left him in the
lurch.

99

## THE CONSONANT SOUND [dʒ]-/dʒ/-(j)

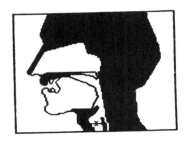
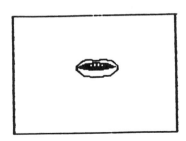

## DESCRIPTION

The phoneme [dʒ]-/dʒ/-(j) is the voiced tongue-front to front-palate africate consonant. It is produced in the following manner:
1. The front of the tongue is placed against the front-palate, blocking the breath stream.
2. The mouth is nearly closed.
3. The lips are rounded and pushed forward.
4. Air is exhaled and passes through the closed vocal folds causing phonation.
5. The voiced air stream builds up pressure.
6. The tongue is lowered slightly, allowing the air to explode from the mouth.
7. The breath stream is forced between the tongue and the palate.

## SPELLINGS

The [dʒ]-/dʒ/-(j) sound is spelled in these ways:

"dge" as in "judge"          "di" as in "soldier"
"g" as in "general"          "gg" as in "suggest"
              "j" as in "juice"

## PROBLEMS

The [dʒ]-/dʒ/-(j) sound may be replaced by the [tʃ]-/tʃ/-(ch) so that "jump" sounds like "chump." A sound may be added to the [dʒ]-/dʒ/-(j) at the ends of words so that "cage" sounds like "cagey". Other substitutions include [d], so that "Jean" sounds like "dean," [z], so that "juice" seems like "Zeus," and [j]-/y/-(y), so that "jet" sounds like "yet."

100

[ dʒ ]                           /dʒ/                                j

## PRACTICE A - WORDS

| General | Jet | arranGed | danGer | aGe | eDGe |
|---------|-----|----------|--------|-----|------|
| Gentle | Job | briDGes | **enGine** | chanGe | knowleDGe |
| German | Join | challenGes | maJor | colleGe | larGe |
| January | Jump | caGes | solDIers | couraGe | paGe |
| Japan | Just | charGing | suGGest | damaGe | **villaGe** |

## PRACTICE B - CONTRASTS

| | | |
|---|---|---|
| Jeans-dean's | charGe-chars | Jet-yet |
| Gym-dim | Jeep-**cheap** | eDGe-edgy |
| Jade-shade | eDGing-etching | weDGe-wedgy |
| Jail-shale | baDGe-batch | huGe-hue |
| Juice-Zeus | Jaw-yaw | sieGe-see |

## PRACTICE C - SENTENCE CONTRASTS

1. Dean's Jeans are red.
2. That's a dim Gym.
3. There's a shale Jail.
4. I got a cheep Jeep.
5. I'm eDGing an etching.
6. He'll ride a Jet, yet.
7. Ray is in a raGe.
8. I'm edgy on the eDGE.
9. I'll see the sieGe.
10. It will surGe, sir.

## PRACTICE D - SENTENCES

1. In general the American judicial system is just.
2. Wise judges and good juries make it work.
3. Most dangerous criminals spend time in jail.
4. Intelligent lawyers generally see justice done.
5. Gorgeous Georgia, is a personal injury lawyer.
6. Jack, her husband, is a courageous judge.
7. Jack never judges Georgia's trials.
8. Where Georgia is concerned, Jack is generous.
9. Jack suggests other judges for Georgia's cases.
10. Therefore Georgia and Jack enjoy their marriage.

### TONGUE TWISTER

James, Jim, and Jack,
born in January,
courageously managed
marriage with Jane,
Jean and Joan, born in
June, in July.

### LIMERICK

A thief, whose name is Mudge,
Took, from a lady, her fudge.
Said the jury, "We know
To jail Mudge must go."
Said the judge: "from jail
      Mudge won't budge."

## THE CONSONANT SOUND [hw]-/hw/-(hw)

 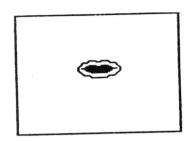

### DESCRIPTION

The phoneme [hw] is the voiceless lip-to-lip glide consonant. It is produced in the following manner:
1. The mouth is nearly closed.
2. The lips are tightly rounded, somewhat like the position for the sound [u]-/uʏ-(o͞o).
3. Air is exhaled through the open vocal folds.
4. The voiceless breath stream passes through the rounded lips.
5. The lips are then moved to the position for the vowel which follows in the word being uttered.

### SPELLINGS

The following spelling results in the [hw] sound:

"wh" as in "where"

### PROBLEMS

The primary problem with the [hw] sound is that of substitution. The phoneme [v] may replace it so that "whale" sounds like "veil," or "wheel" sounds like "veal." The [w] may be used, so that "where" sounds like "wear," or "which" sounds like "witch."

[hw]                    /hw/                       hw

## PRACTICE A - WORDS

| | | | | |
|---|---|---|---|---|
| WHale | WHeat | WHether | WHistle | everyWHere |
| WHat | WHeel | WHich | WHite | noWHere |
| WHat's | WHen | WHile | WHy | someWHat |
| WHatever | WHere | WHisper | anyWHere | someWHere |

## PRACTICE B - CONTRASTS

| | | |
|---|---|---|
| WHale-veil | WHale-wail | WHet-wet |
| WHeel-veal | WHere-wear | WHey-way |
| WHile-vile | Whether-weather | WHile-wile |
| WHine-vine | Wheel-we'll | WHich-witch |
| Why-vie. | WHeeled-wield | WHy-Y |

## PRACTICE C - SENTENCE CONTRASTS

1. Buy a WHale veil.
2. WHy do you vie?
3. Does a WHale wail?
4. We'll buy a WHeel.
5. You'll wear it WHere?
6. WHet it when wet.
7. The WHigs wore wigs.
8. Don't WHine for wine.
9. WHich witch is here?
10. WHy has a "y" in it.

## PRACTICE D - SENTENCES

1. Reporters ask: "where, when, who, what and why".
2. We want to know what happened and where it was.
3. We want to know when it was and why it happened.
4. "Somewhere" and "anywhere" aren't good enough.
5. "When", "why", "what" and "where" are the news.
6. Newsman Al White forgot which questions to ask.
7. White forgot "what", "where", "why" and "when".
8. When White started to write, he had no facts.
9. White whistled while the boss read his story.
10. Now White knows what to ask when a story breaks.

### TONGUE TWISTER

We while away time whistling and whittling. Nowhere are there more whistlers and whittlers than here.

### LIMERICK

White water rafting is fun,
When whizzing down in the sun.
While floating along
And whistling a song,
You relax on a white water run.

## THE CONSONANT SOUND [w]-/w/-(w)

 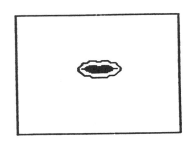

## DESCRIPTION

The phoneme [w] is the voiced lip-to-lip glide consonant. It is produced in the following manner:

1. The mouth is nearly closed.
2. The lips are tightly rounded, somewhat like the position for the sound [u]-/u͞/-(o͞o).
3. Air is exhaled through the closed vocal folds, causing vibration.
4. The vibrated air passes through the rounded lips.
5. The lips are then moved to the position for the vowel which follows in the word being uttered.
6. The resulting sound is similar to producing an [u]-/u͞/-(o͞o) followed by a vowel.

## SPELLINGS

The following spellings result in the [w] sound:

> "o", as in "one"
> "oi", as in "reservoir"
> "u" as in "queen"
> "w" as in "water"

## PROBLEMS

The primary problem with the [w] sound is that of substitution. The phoneme [v] may replace it so that "went" sounds like "vent," or "we're" sounds like "veer." Less frequently, the [r] may intrude so that "wide" sounds like "ride." The [g] is sometimes used so that "wood" sounds similar to "good."

[w]                              /w/                              w

## PRACTICE A - WORDS

| Wait | Was   | We   | Will  | alWays    | forWard  |
|------|-------|------|-------|-----------|----------|
| Wall | Watch | Week | With  | aWay      | qUestion |
| Want | Water | Well | Word  | betWeen   | qUick    |
| War  | Wave  | Went | Work  | eqUal     | qUiet    |
| Warm | Way   | Were | Would | everyOne  | someOne  |

## PRACTICE B - CONTRASTS

| Wail-veil      | West-vest    | Walk-gawk   |
|----------------|--------------|-------------|
| Weird-veered   | Wet-vet      | Wall-gall   |
| We'll-veal     | Wait-rate    | West-guest  |
| Went-vent      | Went-rent    | Wise-guise  |
| We're-veer     | Wide-ride    | Wood-good   |

## PRACTICE C - SENTENCE CONTRASTS

1.  We'll not eat veal.
2.  He Went to the vent.
3.  The vet got Wet.
4.  Wait for a good rate.
5   I Went for the rent.
6.  You Wait by the gate.
7.  Don't Walk and gawk.
8.  My guest went West.
9.  I Won a gun.
10. That's good Wood.

## PRACTICE D - SENTENCES

1.  Weather is one thing everyone worries about.
2.  Walter Williams is a weatherman.
3.  Walter's work is to give weather reports on TV.
4.  Wanda, Walter's wife, writes weather reports.
5.  One day, Walter said the weather would be good.
6.  Wanda wrote that the weather would be wild.
7.  Everyone wondered what the weather would be.
8.  The way it was, no one needed to worry.
9.  Wanda's and Walter's weather reports were right.
10. It was warm in the morning and wet in the night.

### TONGUE TWISTER

A wily wolf waited
for a wild rabbit to
walk his way.  One
wild one went by but
the wolf was napping
and awakened late.

### LIMERICK

A wicked old witch at the zoo
Wanted to make wombat stew.
The wombat attacked her.
It wildly whacked her,
So the witch made her stew with
    a gnu.

105

THE CONSONANT SOUND [j]-/y/-(y)

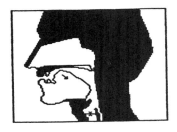 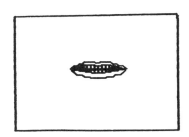

## DESCRIPTION

The phoneme [j]-/y/-(y) is the voiced tongue-blade to front-palate glide consonant. It is produced in the following manner:
1. The tongue-blade is raised close to, but not touching the front-palate. Its position is like that of the high front vowels.
2. The mouth is slightly open.
3. Air is exhaled through the lightly closed vocal folds, causing phonation.
4. As the voiced air passes through the mouth, the tongue and jaw move to the position for the vowel which follows the [j]-/y/-(y) sound.

## SPELLINGS

The [j]-/y/-(y) sound in spelled in these ways:

> "ea" as in "beauty"
> "eu" as in "feud"
> "ew" as in "few"
> "gn" as in "vignette"
> "i" as in "onion"
> "ie" as in "view"
> "u" as in "use"
> "ue" as in "fuel"
> "y" as in "yes"

## PROBLEMS

The primary problem with the [j]-/y/-(y) sound is that of substitution. The phoneme [dʒ]-/dʒ/-(j) may replace it so that "yes" sounds like "Jess," or "you'll" sounds like "jewel."

[j]                    /y/                         y

## PRACTICE A - WORDS

| | | | | | |
|---|---|---|---|---|---|
| Europe | Useful | Yes | argUe | fEw | hUman |
| UnIt | Usual | You | bEAuty | fIgUre | IndIan |
| United | Yard | Young | continUe | fUel | mUsic |
| University | Year | Your | cUbe | fUture | pUre |
| Use | Yell | Youth | cUrious | hUge | vIEw |

## PRACTICE B - CONTRASTS

| | | |
|---|---|---|
| Yacht-jot | Year-jeer | Yet-jet |
| Yak-jack | Yell-jell | Yip-gyp |
| Yale-jail | Yelled-jelled | Yolk-joke |
| Yam-jam | Yellow-jello | Yowl-jowl |
| Yard-jarred | Yes-Jess | Use-juice |

## PRACTICE C - SENTENCE CONTRASTS

1. Jack rode a Yak.         6. Jess said: "Yes."
2. I'm in the Yale jail.    7. No jet is here, Yet.
3. Jay said: "Yea."         8. That Yolk is a joke.
4. Don't jeer all Year.     9. You'll see the jewel.
5  The jello is Yellow.    10. I've no Use for juice.

## PRACTICE D - SENTENCES

1.  Your youthful years should be used with care.
2.  The younger you are, the easier you can learn.
3.  Most youthful years are spent as a student.
4.  The young don't enjoy youth until it is used up.
5.  The youth is secure knowing years are ahead.
6.  The useful years of youth are really very few.
7.  Many of the young contribute much to the USA.
8.  They use their young years wisely.
9.  You can insure a good future by studious effort.
10. Useful, youthful years produce useful adult ones.

| TONGUE TWISTER | LIMERICK |
|---|---|

Yesterday's onions      A youth used a new violin.
should not be used      He placed it under his chin.
in the stew. If         The music he made
you used yesterday's    Was beautifully played.
onions, your stew       Years of practice payed off
will be refused.             again.

107

## THE CONSONANT SOUND [l]-/l/-(l)

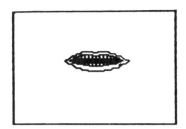

### DESCRIPTION

The phoneme [l] is the voiced tongue-tip to gum-ridge glide lateral consonant. It is produced in the following manner:
1. The tongue-tip is raised to the gum-ridge.
2. The mouth is nearly wide open.
3. The lips are neutral.
4. Air is exhaled through the lightly closed vocal folds, causing phonation.
5. The voiced breath stream is kept from exiting the mouth over the front of the tongue, and is forced around the the tongue's sides.

### SPELLINGS

The following spellings result in the [l] sound:

> "l" as in "look"
> "ll" as in "well"

### PROBLEMS

The most common problems with the phoneme [l] include substitution with the sounds [r] and [n], so that "long" sounds like "wrong," or "roaring" like "rolling," and "lock" sounds like "knock," or "light" like "night."

[1]                              /1/                              1

## PRACTICE A - WORDS

| Land   | Little | aLone   | beLow    | aLL   | stiLL  |
|--------|--------|---------|----------|-------|--------|
| Large  | Line   | aLong   | foLLOw   | caLL  | teLL   |
| Learn  | Live   | aLso    | miLLion  | miLe  | untiL  |
| Letter | Long   | aLways  | onLy     | oiL   | weLL   |
| Like   | Look   | beLieve | suddenLy | smaLL | wiLL   |

## PRACTICE B - CONTRASTS

| Laid-raid | Lock-rock        | Lock-knock | failed-feined |
|-----------|------------------|------------|---------------|
| Late-rate | coLLect-correct  | Let-net    | teller-tenor  |
| Law-raw   | miLes-mires      | Lit-knit   | iLL-in        |
| Lay-ray   | miLLer-mirror    | Lie-nigh   | maiL-main     |
| Lead-read | roLLing-roaring  | Look-nook  | teLL-ten      |

## PRACTICE C - SENTENCE CONTRASTS

1.  We Laughed on a raft.
2.  Ray Lay down.
3.  I read about Lead.
4.  MiLLer has a mirror.
5.  CoLLect correct ones.
6.  Knock by the Lock.
7.  Let me net it.
8.  I need a night Light.
9.  My teLLer is a tenor.
10. MaiL the main one.

## PRACTICE D - SENTENCES

*the person lease.*

1.  Larry Lake is a reliable landlord.
2.  He leases lodgings in a large yellow building.
3.  A lot of people don't like landlords.
4.  Some do little and let buildings fall apart.
5.  They collect rent only and don't solve problems.
6.  Larry allows his lessees to call all the time.
7.  He carefully completes all repairs promptly.
8.  He listens to complaints and looks for problems.
9.  Larry's lessees always feel completely joyful.
10. These lessees never look elsewhere for lodgings.

### TONGUE TWISTER *can't skip*

Little lions like
to leap and lope,
but large lions
like killing.  We
like the little
playful lions.

### LIMERICK

There once was a lady, so tall,
Who learned to play basketball.
Her long legs could leap
And thus she could keep
Her team mates from losing at
all.

109

THE CONSONANT SOUND [r]-/r/-(r)

  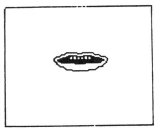

DESCRIPTION

The phoneme [r] is the voiced tongue-center to central-palate glide consonant. It is produced in the following manner:
1. It begins with the tongue in either of the two positions used in the production of the [ɝ]-/ɝr/-(ûr) sound.
   A. With the tongue-tip up, by the front-palate, and its center raised near the center-palate, or:
   B. With the tongue-tip behind the lower front teeth, and its front and center near the central-palate.
2. Air is exhaled through the lightly closed vocal folds, causing phonation.
3. The mouth is half open.
4. The lips are in a neutral position, but their outer edges may be pushed slightly forward.
5. As the phoneme is made, the articulators move immediately to the position for the next sound.

SPELLINGS

The following spellings result in the [r] sound:

"r" as in "run"          "rr" as in "tomorrow"
          "wr" as in "write"

PROBLEMS

The [l] may be substituted for [r], so that "red" sounds like "led," or "berry" like "belly." An [r] made with the tongue tip rapidly moving against the palate (a trilled [r]) is often used. "Carry" would sound somewhat like "caddy."

[ r ]                /r/

*guy — male*
*gal — female*
                                                    r

## PRACTICE A    WORDS

| | | | | |
|---|---|---|---|---|
| Raised | Remain | Right | alReady | diRection |
| Reached | Remember | River | AmeRica | EuRope |
| Read | Represent | Rock | aRound | eveRy |
| Reason | Result | Room | caRRY | eveRyone |
| Red | Return | WRite | diffeRence | eveRything |

## PRACTICE B - CONTRASTS

| | | | |
|---|---|---|---|
| Race-lace | Rear-leer | Rush-lush | eRect-elect |
| Rain-lane | Ride-lied | WRist-list | hiRing-hiding |
| Rake-lake | Right-light | WRong-long | JeRRy-jelly |
| Rate-late | River-liver | boRing-bowling | LaRRy-laddy |
| Read-lead | Room-loom | caRRy-caddy | reReel-redeal |

## PRACTICE C - SENTENCE CONTRASTS

1. Rain fell in a lane.
2. He lied on the Ride.
3. Use the Right light.
4. The WRong one's long.
5. A lush likes to Rush.
6. One Row is too low.
7. JeRRy bought jelly.   *Lassy*
8. Bowling is boRing.
9. The caddy can caRRy.
10. LaRRy's a nice laddy.

*(a)*
*Lady = Leidi*
*← practice.*

## PRACTICE D - SENTENCES

1. Myra is a responsible radio reporter.  *←*
2. She rides around the city looking for robberies.
3. One January, police raided a robbers room.
4. Myra ran in as the robber fired his rifle.
5. Injuries rapidly resulted, but Myra was alright.
6. She rapped the robber's head with her radio.
7. She wrestled for the robbers dangerous rifle.
8. He roared and raved, but she ripped it from him.
9. With the robber arrested, Myra wrote her story.
10. Myra's real experience was correctly reported.

TONGUE TWISTER

Around and around
ran the red rooster.
"Run, run, the river
is rising," he   *zi*
crowed.  "The Rogue
River is rolling!"
   *(a)*
   *red*

LIMERICK

"The reason I carry a rope,"
Roared   sheriff, Roger McCope,
"Is to rope, with its loop,
A rustler named Roop.
He's robbed his last ranch, is
    my hope."

111

## THE CONSONANT SOUND [m]-/m/-(m)

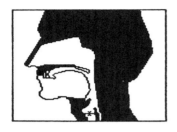
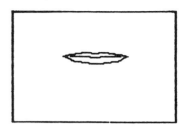

### DESCRIPTION

The phoneme [m] is the voiced lip-to-lip nasal consonant. It is produced in the following manner:
1. The tongue is in a neutral position.
2. The upper and lower lips come together preventing air from exiting the mouth.
3. The soft palate is lowered, opening the nasal passages.
4. Air is exhaled through the lightly closed vocal folds, causing phonation.
5. Voiced air passes through the nose.

### SPELLINGS

The following spellings result in the [m] sound:

"m" as in "may"
"mb" as in "thumb"
"mn" as in "condemn"

### PROBLEMS

The primary difficulty with the [m] is omission. It is frequently dropped from the ends of words so that "home" sounds like "hoe," or "time" like "tie."

[m]                    /m/                        m

## PRACTICE A - WORDS

| Made | Means | AMerican | nuMber | caMe | naMe |
| Make | More | coMplete | reMeMber | forM | saMe |
| Man | Most | exaMple | seeMed | froM | soMe |
| Many | Much | hiMself | sMall | hiM | theM |
| May | Most | iMportant | soMething | hoMe | tiMe |

## PRACTICE B - CONTRASTS

| booM-boo | faMe-Fay | miMe-my | seeM-see |
| caMe-Kay | foaM-foe | gnoMe-no | teaM-tea |
| daMe-day | hoMe-hoe | rhyMe-rye | tiMe-tie |
| diMe-dye | I'M-I | roaM-roe | toMe-toe |
| doMe-dough | maiM-may | saMe-say | whoM-who |

## PRACTICE C - SENTENCE CONTRASTS

1. Kay caMe home.
2. The dye is a diMe.
3. Put foaM on the foe.
4. A gnoMe said: "No."
5. He may maiM you.
6. I'M glad I can go.
7. Say the saMe thing.
8. I see the seaM.
9. The teaM had herb tea.
10. Ask "whoM", not "who".

## PRACTICE D - SENTENCES

1. Mack and Mary wanted more muscles.
2. Making mighty muscles was important to Mack.
3. His muscles were too small to make him complete.
4. Mary didn't want big muscles, but to be slim.
5. Mack and Mary commenced attending a gym.
6. Aerobics made Mary make many movements to music.
7. Mack moved a mountain of massive weights.
8. Mary slimmed down and improved her form.
9. Mack's muscles became massive.
10. Mack became a movie stunt man and Mary a model.

### TONGUE TWISTER

Remember to remove
muddy mittens
before coming home.
Mud makes homes
more messy then
Moms want them.

### LIMERICK

A woman from Rome had a dream
That she sewed a majestic seam.
She made many messes,
Then magnificent dresses.
Now money in her hand does
    gleam.

113

## THE CONSONANT SOUND [n]-/n/-(n)

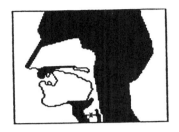
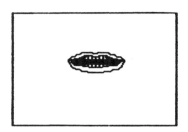

DESCRIPTION

The phoneme [n] is the voiced tongue-tip to gum-ridge nasal consonant. It is made in the following manner:
1. The tongue-tip is raised to the gum-ridge. The sides of the tongue seal against the teeth and block the air from exiting the mouth.
2. The mouth is half open.
3. The lips are neutral.
4. The soft palate is lowered, opening the nasal passages.
5. Air is exhaled through the lightly closed vocal folds, causing phonation.
6. The voiced breath stream passes out of the nose.

SPELLINGS

The following spellings result in the [n] sound:

"gn" as in "gnostic"
"kn" as in "knee"
"mn" as in "mnemonic"
"pn" as in "pneumatic"
"n" as in "new"
"nn" as in "sunny"
"sn" as in "demesne"

PROBLEMS

The most common problem with the phoneme [n] is omission. It is often not produced at the ends of words, so that "sane" sounds like "say," or "bean" like "bee."

[n]                    /n/                          n

## PRACTICE A - WORDS

| KNow  | New  | aNd     | eNd   | aN    | oN   |
|-------|------|---------|-------|-------|------|
| Name  | Next | aNimal  | iNto  | caN   | oNe  |
| Near  | Not  | aNother | maNy  | dowN  | thaN |
| Need  | No   | aNswer  | oNly  | iN    | theN |
| Never | Now  | aNy     | poiNt | learN | wheN |

## PRACTICE B - CONTRASTS

| baNe-bay  | phoNe-foe | leaN-lea | moaN-mow  |
|-----------|-----------|----------|-----------|
| beaN-be   | gaiN-gay  | liNe-lie | nooN-new  |
| boNe-Bo   | hoNe-hoe  | loaN-low | seeN-sea  |
| coiN-coy  | joiN-joy  | maiN-may | sewN-so   |
| diNe-die  | laiN-lay  | meaN-me  | tuNe-too  |

## PRACTICE C - SENTENCE CONTRASTS

1. It may be a beaN.
2. Bo broke a boNe.
3. Don't phoNe the foe.
4. Please hoNe the hoe.
5. Joy will joiN you.
6. We may leave MaiNe.
7. It'll lie on the liNe.
8. He's meaN to me.
9. I've seeN the sea.
10. Sing a tuNe or two.

## PRACTICE D - SENTENCES

1. Nina was a night nurse at a nursing home.
2. She also nursed children in a day care center.
3. Nina needed a nap between her two employments.
4. Next to Nina's apartment lived a noisy person.
5. The man, a musician, **played pianos and horns.**
6. Nina's nap time was when he sounded his horn.
7. Nina couldn't stand it another afternoon.
8. She went to the man and knocked on his window.
9. She noticed, then, that he was a handsome man.
10. Nina needs no naps, now; she listens to horns

### TONGUE TWISTER

Near noon, nine
ninnies knealed
on the ground and
nibbled on lunch.
They crunched and
munched noisily.

### LIMERICK

A scientist once went to dine
At nearly a quarter to nine.
He noticed, on a bean,
A insect, very green,
Which he soon pickled in brine.

## THE CONSONANT SOUND [ŋ]–/ŋ/–⟨nǧ⟩

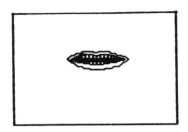

### DESCRIPTION

The phoneme [ŋ]–/ŋ/–⟨nǧ⟩ is the voiced tongue-back to soft palate nasal consonant. It is made in the following manner:
1. The back of the tongue is raised to the soft palate, blocking the exit of air through the mouth.
2. The mouth is half open.
3. The lips are neutral.
4. The soft palate is lowered.
5. Air is exhaled through the lightly closed vocal folds, causing phonation.
6. The voiced breath stream is kept from exiting the mouth by the tongue and is forced to pass through the nose.

### SPELLINGS

The [ŋ]–/ŋ/–⟨nǧ⟩ sound is spelled in these ways:

> "n" as in "rancor"
> "nch" as in "anchor"
> ng" as in "sing"
> "nk" as in "link"
> "nqu" as in "conquer"

### PROBLEMS

Several sounds are substituted for the sound [ŋ]–/ŋ/–⟨nǧ⟩. The sound [n] is used, so that "singing" sounds like "sinning," or "ding" like "din." The [m] sound may intrude so that "sang" sounds like "Sam." The [g] is heard, so that "bring" sounds like "brig." Sometimes, the [g] is added to the end of a word.

116

**[ŋ]**　　　　　　/ŋ/　　　　　　　　　　nᵍ

## PRACTICE A - WORDS

| | | | | |
|---|---|---|---|---|
| aNGer | leNGth | aloNG | duriNG | loNG |
| briNGing | siNGle | anythiNG | everythiNG | morniNG |
| eNGlish | siNGing | beginniNG | feeliNG | siNG |
| fiNGer | thiNGs | beloNG | followiNG | somethiNG |
| haNGs | thiNk | burniNG | huntiNG | spriNG |

## PRACTICE B - CONTRASTS

| | | | |
|---|---|---|---|
| toNGues-tons | thiNG-thin | wiNGs-wigs | briNGs-brims |
| siNGer-sinner | toNGue-ton | haNG-hag | riNGs-rims |
| wiNGs-wins | wiNG-win | saNG-sag | swiNGs-swims |
| kiNG-kin | luNGs-lugs | riNG-rig | briNG-brim |
| suNG-sun | toNGues-tugs | taNG-tag | haNG-ham |

## PRACTICE C - SENTENCE CONTRASTS

1. She runs up ruNGs.
2. He wins his wiNGs.
3. The kiNG has kin.
4. I've suNG in the sun.
5. That's a thin thiNG.
6. We must rig the riNG.
7. I wraNG the rag.
8. She swiNGs and swims.
9. BriNG it to the brim.
10. HaNG up the ham.

## PRACTICE D - SENTENCES

1. Human beings enjoy doing something.
2. Doing nothing is frustrating and tiring.
3. Doing anything's more satisfying than nothing
4. We like walking, running, playing and watching.
5. Cooking, reading, writing and dancing are fun.
6. Having nothing to do, however, is frustrating.
7. It's irritating, exasperating and maddening.
8. Even relaxing means doing something.
9. Sleeping and dreaming are not doing nothing.
10. Working, playing and resting make happy beings.

### TONGUE TWISTER

A singer broke some
fingers catching
falling song books.
Breaking fingers is
more irritating if
your bowling.

### LIMERICK

A gonger from the city of Kong,
Rings gongs for many a song.
If the wrong gong is rung,
The wrong song is sung.
A wrong gonger won't ring gongs
for long.

117

## SUMMARY

Each of the 25 consonants is significant in the correct pronunciation of English. The five consonant categories (plosives, fricatives, africates, glides and nasals) are produced with different manners of articulation. Each consonant has its own place of articulation and type of voicing.

Some of these sounds are not in your first language. Some of them are similar to your old sounds, but are used differently, such as at the ends of words. Making these phonemes become habitual in your speech will require that you slow down as you speak to give yourself time to move your articulators in the correct manner. As always, this will require PRACTICE, PRACTICE AND MORE PRACTICE.

# CHAPTER 7

# BLENDING SOUNDS

It would be relatively easy to learn English pronunciation were it not for the problems of vowel-r, diphthong-r and consonant-consonant blends. This joining together and combining of certain phonemes requires special attention and practice.

## VOWEL-R AND DIPHTHONG-R BLENDS

Many of the vowels and diphthongs blend with the [r] sound to form what might be considered a separate phonemes. Consider the interjective "bah", indicating something disliked. With the letter "r" added it becomes "bar." Note that if you say "bah", your mouth stays open momentarily, holding on to the [ɑ]-/ɑ/-(ä-ŏ) sound. If you say "bar", however, your articulators don't pause at all, but rapidly move through the [ɑ]-/ɑ/-(ä-ŏ) on their way to [ɝ]-/ɘr/-(ûr) (the stopping point of the "r"). If you say the words "knee" and "near", or "flow" and "floor", you will note the same pattern: rather than a pure vowel sound, the vowel is changed by the addition of the "r".

For many students of American English pronunciation, some of these combinations can be very difficult to say. For example, it is relatively easy to learn to produce [ɛ]-/ɛ/-(ĕ), and a bit harder to master [ɝ]-/ɘr/-(ûr), but [ɛr]-/ɛr/-(âr) is much harder to say than either sound alone.

119

## CONSONANT-CONSONANT BLENDS

Consonants are often blended with other consonants, with no vowel between them. Consider, for example, the word "blue". To pronounce it, the articulators first are moved to the position for [b]. As it is being exploded, they are shifted immediately to the position for [l]. They then are moved to the position of the vowel, [u]–/uỹ–⟨o͞o⟩. There is no sound or space between the phonemes [b] and [l].

Look at the words "try", "sweater," "clock", and "length". Each of these contains two different consonants blended to form what is, almost, a separate, new sound.

There are some words which contain three consonants blended together. Look at the words "street" and "fifths". Each contains three consonant sounds in a row, with no intervening vowel. Some of these blends are especially difficult, since they contain one or more phonemes which are quite difficult to learn alone.

## BLEND PRACTICE

The next several pages contain practice material for the various blends. It is arranged somewhat differently from that of the previous chapters. The vowel blends will be combined into one single lesson and the consonant blends into another. No word or sentence contrasts will be presented and sentences will combine several blends together.

## PRACTICE A - WORDS

**[ɪr]** /ɪər/ îr
EAR    EARdrum    chEERful    nEARby    bEER    hERE

**[ɛr]** /ɛəʋ/ âr
AIR    AIRport    CAREful    dARED    bEAR    thERE
AIRplane    AIRtight    chAIRs    hAIRcut    hAIR    whERE

**[ɑr]** /ɑr/ är
ARe    ARch    dARk    mARk    CAR    jAR
ARc    ARm    hARd    shARp    fAR    stAR

**[ɔr]** /ɔr/ ôr
ORchestra    ORgan    cORner    hORse    dOOR    mORE
ORder    ORient    cOURt    shORt    flOOR    sORE

**[ʊr]** /ʊər/ ŏor
EURope    yOURself    lURE    tOUR    yOUR

**[ɑɪr]** /ɑɪər/ īr
IRE    IRoned    chOIRs    tIREd    entIRE    lIAR
IRon    IRoning    fIREs    wIRes    inquIRE    retIRE

**[ɑʊr]** /ɑʊər/ our
HOUR    OUR    bOWERs    shOWERs    flOUR    pOWER

## PRACTICE B - SENTENCES

1. A fireman gets tired fighting a four hour fire.
2. His daring job requires very hard, careful work.
3. Firemen wear their hair short for fear of fire.
4. Larry Hart is a  wiry, short haired fireman.
5. Larry fought four terrible fires in four hours.
6. Hart had worked hard and was very tired.
7. When you're tired, your carefulness disappears.
8. In a flower shop fire, some iron fell on a wire.
9. Big sparks roared up, near Larry's ear.
10. His short hair didn't flare; Hart is still here.

### TONGUE TWISTER

Care for yourself
in airports.  Armed
guards and alarms
in doors are hard,
but you're sure to
be more secure.

### LIMERICK

You're sure to stand and cheer
When you order your food here.
Our short order cook
Makes his food to look
Like it hasn't been sitting all
     year.

121

# The Pronunciation of Standard American English

## PRACTICE A - WORDS

Blends with [d] as the second element:

| rubbed | bagged | changed | yelled | hand | hanged |
| sobbed | tagged | judged | hummed | wind | bathed |

Blends with [l] as first element.

| bulb | cold | bulge | film | else | health |
| gulch | golf | silk | help | salt | solve |

Blends with [l] as the second element:

| blend | flag | glad | class | play | slip |
| blue | fly | glue | clear | please | slow |

Blends with [m], [n], and [ŋ]-(ng) as the first element:

| jump | stamp | bench | ranch | thank | change |
| lamp | stump | inch | ink | think | range |

Blends with [r] as the second element:

| bread | draw | free | cry | shrub | three |
| brown | dream | grow | pray | tree | through |

Blends with [s] as the first element:

| school | ask | smell | snow | wasp | star |
| sky | small | snap | spell | rest | stop |

## PRACTICE B - SENTENCES

1. The film industry hasn't made many changes.
2. Its techniques and its equipment have changed.
3. Its purposes are practically identical.
4. The film business wants to entertain people.
5. It likes laughter, crying, and shrieking.
6. The gulches of old "westerns" are city canyons.
7. The slapstick of the past is still acceptable.
8. The computerized film isn't more suspenseful.
9. Film's snow is still bright, and its sky's blue.
10. We still clap when the brave crush the crooked.

| TONGUE TWISTER | LIMERICK |

A quick, quiet brown faced landlord rents tents to healthy, wealthy, dreamy blue eyed blonds and brown skinned brunettes.

Queen Gwen, the 4th, of Spain, Traveled to Greece by train. Gwen ate just brown bread. And slept badly in bed. Now she only travels by plane.

122

## PRACTICE A - WORDS

Blends with [s] as the second element:

| beliefs | breaks | sense | keeps | eats | baths |
| safes | box | tense | wipes | notes | breaths |

Blends with [t] as the second element:

| laughed | act | can't | accept | pressed | cashed |
| soft | liked | rent | hoped | test | brushed |

Blends with [θ]-(th) as the second element:

| breadth | filth | stealth | month | fifteenth | length |
| width | health | wealth | tenth | sixteenth | strength |

Blends with [w] as the second element:

| quart | quick | twenty | twirl | swat | swell |

Blends with [z] as the second element:

| cabs | beds | drags | games | brains | breathes |
| cribs | leads | tells | times | lense | saves |

Blends with three consonants together:

| scratch | holds | films | blends | lists | lengths |
| spray | gulfs | helps | thinks | wrists | fifths |
| street | bulged | malts | asks | breadths | sixths |

## PRACTICE B - SENTENCES

1. Trucks, cars, vans, and cabs need to be fueled.
2. They must be oiled, cleaned, and lubricated.
3. Frank's Friendly Truck Stop gives quick help.
4. All needs are fulfilled with kindly smiles.
5. Frank's tested and trusted crew is trained.
6. Honesty and integrity are Frank's watchwords.
7. If you're stranded by a broken engine, he helps.
8. Your car is fixed quickly and inexpensively.
9. All work's completly tested and never rejected.
10. Don't you wish that an actual Frank's existed?

### TONGUE TWISTER

By the tenth of the
month, the electric,
rent and plastic bills
must be mailed or
you'll be disconected,
ejected and rejected.

### LIMERICK

Fred is a scribbler of lists,
Writing with both his fists.
He's scratching so fast,
We don't think he'll last.
He'll soon have splints on
his wrists.

SUMMARY

There are two major types of blends, vowel-[r] and diphthong-[r] blends and consonant-consonant. Blended sounds cause a special problem for the learner of English. Joining two sounds together usually alters them both slightly, so that a new sound must be learned.

Practice the blend lessons carefully. Take your time. Be certain to produce each phoneme in the blend exactly. The [r] blends require extra effort to be certain that the [ɝ]–/ɚr/–⟨ûr⟩ part of each word is heard, as in "care" and "more."

# CHAPTER 8

# ADDING ENDINGS

A constant problem in English pronunciation is the addition of "ed" and "s," or "es" endings to words for various grammatical purposes. Without study, it is difficult to determine how these letters should be pronounced.

## THE "ED" ENDINGS

Consider the following verbs: "rake," "play," and "wait." The letters "ed" are added to make third person singular past tense. The words become "raked", "played," and "waited." They are pronounced as follows: [rekt]-(rākt), [pled]-(plād), and [wetId]-(wātid). The three ending sounds in the past tense are different: a [t], a [d] and an [ɪd]-/ɪd/-(ĭd).

## THE "ED" RULES

The pronunciation of "ed" endings is determined by three rules which relate to the last sound of the verb in the present tense. Note the three words again. If you looked them up in a dictionary, you would find that "rake" ends with [k], a voiceless phoneme. "Play" ends with the vowel [e]-/eʸ/-(ā), a voiced sound. The last sound in "wait" is [t], a voiceless sound, but a tongue-tip to gum-ridge plosive. These facts point to the "ed" pronunciation rules:

1. If the present tense ending is voiceless,
   "ed" = [t]
2. If the present tense ending is voiced,
   "ed" = [d].
3. If the present tense ending is [t] or [d]
   (both tongue-tip to gum-ridge plosives),
   "ed" = [ɪd]-/ɪd/-(ĭd).

## THE "S" ENDINGS

An "s," or "es" is added to words to make plural nouns, "noun + is" contractions, possessives and regular third person singular present tense verbs.

Now, consider the following words: "seat," "leave," and "kiss." Their ending sounds are respectively: [t], a voiceless sound, [v], a voiced one, and [z], one of six sounds called <u>sibilants</u> ([s], [z], [ʃ]-/ʃ/-(sh), [ʒ]-/ʒ/-(zh), [tʃ]-/tʃ-(ch), and [dʒ]-/dʒ/-(j). With "s" or "es" added, these words become: "seats," "leaves," and "kisses." They are pronounced: [sɪts]-(sĭts), [livz]-(lēvz), and and ['kɪsɪz]-(kĭs'ĭz). Their endings are: [s], [z], and [ɪz]-/ɪz/-(ĭz), respectively. Examining them leads leads to the "s" rules.

## THE "S" RULES

These are quite similar to the "ed" rules.

1. If the word ending is voiceless,
   "s" (or "es") = [s].
2. If the word ending is voiced,
   "s" (or "es") = [z].
3. If the word ending is one of the six
   sibilants (see above),
   "s" (or "es") = [ɪz]-/ɪz/-(ĭz).

## APPLYING THE RULES

These rules may seem complicated at first, but they become easier with practice. Your primary problem is determining the ending of the original word. Try your skill on the practice page.

## PRACTICE A - "ED" ENDINGS

| [t] | | [d] | | [ɪd]-(ĭd) | |
|---|---|---|---|---|---|
| asked | laughed | cried | payed | batted | needed |
| based | missed | dreamed | ruled | beaded | rated |
| guessed | raced | moved | toured | grounded | tested |
| joked | watched | neared | used | lifted | wanted |

## PRACTICE B - "ES" AND "S" ENDINGS

### Third Person Singular Verbs and Contractions

| [s] | | [z] | | [ɪz]-(ĭz) | |
|---|---|---|---|---|---|
| asks | makes | breathes | needs | cashes | preaches |
| breaks | puts | drives | pulls | dances | raises |
| hopes | sleeps | hands | tries | judges | uses |
| it's | soap's | he's | Von's | nurse's | watch's |

### Plural Nouns and Possessives

| aunts | paths | birds | lables | dishes | peaches |
|---|---|---|---|---|---|
| books | racks | curves | plans | faces | ranches |
| gifts | safes | Germans | rivers | fuses | ranges |
| Pat's | troop's | John's | Wong's | nurse's | zebra's |

## PRACTICE D - SENTENCES

1. Nurses are needed as workers in hospitals.
2. Once doctors treat patients, nurses are called.
3. Nelly's a night nurse and works odd hours.
4. She's worked for years in the city's hospitals.
5. She's carried, fetched, lifted and cared.
6. She's bathed, clothed and loved her patients.
7. Folks have liked her because she's liked them.
8. She's cared for artists, lawyers and teachers.
9. Golfers, crooks and cops are ones she's helped.
10. It's nice to be among needed and wanted nurses.

### TONGUE TWISTER

It pleased teachers
minds when tested
students results
looked like students
had studied, not
goofed and lazed.

### LIMERICK

The cheese Poles think's swell,
Looks great, until you smell.
It once smelled so bad,
The Poles hired a lad
Who carried it to Russians
 to sell.

127

## SUMMARY

The adding of endings to English words can cause problems to the learner of the language. Knowing the rules for "ed" and "s" endings and using the dictionary will be helpful in determining proper pronunciation.

This is the last lesson in the text. If you have gone through each of them once, you are just beginning in the development of your pronunciation. As has been said before, slow, careful and frequent practice is the key to your improvement.

# USING CASSETTE RECORDERS

An audio cassette recorder is almost a requirement for anyone trying to learn the pronunciation of a new language. It allows you to record and listen to model speakers and to record and play back your own speech. Commercially produced recordings are available for this, and other books, which will provide you with good practice models.

## SELECTING THE RECORDER

Cassette recorders are available in all price ranges and qualities. For strictly voice recording, less expensive equipment is effective. You do not need the most costly recorder, but should be wary of the cheapest.

If you are going to purchase a recorder for speech practice, try it out in the store to be sure that it will perform well. Most modern recorders come with a built in microphone. For many activities, the built in microphone will suffice, but for serious practice, they do not perform well. They tend to record the noise of the machine's motors. We suggest that you use a recorder with an external microphone. If it does not come with one, be sure you can add one later, if you wish.

## USING THE RECORDER

Cassette recorders are useful for speech improvement in several ways:

1.  Your teacher may want you, or allow you, to record material in the classroom which you can practice at home.
2.  You may be assigned to record material at home for your teacher to evaluate.
3.  You may wish to practice lessons from class, or in the book, at home.
4.  You may wish to practice speaking assignments at home before giving them in class.
5.  You may wish to use pre-recorded lesson material, such as the cassettes for this book, or others, at home.
6.  You may wish to record the speech of someone to use in your practice, such as radio or television personalities.

## USING PRE-RECORDED CASSETTES

Pre-recorded cassettes should only be used when you are ready for them. For example, if you have not learned a particular sound yet, your practicing it wrong may make it harder to learn it correctly. Once you have learned it in the classroom, however, home practice will be invaluable to your speech improvement.

When listening to and repeating cassettes you have purchased, recorded in the classroom, or from speakers you admire, you will find it helpful if you can also record the model voice along with yours. You will then be able to compare the result. This can be accomplished using two cassette recorders or a dual cassette recorder (one with the ability to record and play two cassettes at once).

The pre-recorded cassette should be placed in one machine (or on the play side of a dual cassette unit). A blank cassette should be put into the second recorder (or the record side of the dual unit). You should then push the play button for the pre-recorded cassette and the record button for the blank one. Using a microphone, place it near the

130

playing machine. Record its voice. Then speak into it yourself, recording your voice. Then, stop the machines, rewind the recording unit, and listen to the model, followed by your copy. You can then compare the two. You can then continue with the lesson, or repeat parts of it as often as you wish.

Abdominal muscles - 5
Adding endings - 125
Africates - 65, 98, 100
Alphabets - 10
American Heritage Dictionary - 3, 11, 12, 13, 17
Articulating speech sounds - 8
Articulating system - 5, 6
Audio cassette recorder - 129
Audio Cassettes - 4, 129, 130
Blends - 119, 120-124
Breathing system - 5, 6
Center-palate - 7, 48, 50, 110
Cognates - 66
Consonant-consonant blends, 120, 122, 123
Consonants - 11, 13, 14, 63-124, 119, 120
Contractions - 126
Diacritic marks - 10
Diphthong-R blends - 119, 121
Diphthongs - 11, 12, 53-62, 119
Dual-cassette recorder - 130
"ED" endings - 125-127
"ED" rules - 125, 126
Element - 53
"ES" rules - -126
"ES" endings 125-127
Fricatives - 63, 80, 82, 84, 86, 88, 90, 92, 94, 96
Front-palate - 7, 28, 30, 32, 34,  36, 92, 94, 98,
              100, 106
Glides - 102, 104, 106, 108, 110